The Super Simple Guide to Housetraining

REVISED EDITION
Teoti Anderson

T.F.H. Publications
President/CEO: Glen S. Axelrod
Executive Vice President: Mark E. Johnson
Publisher: Christopher T. Reggio
Production Manager: Kathy Bontz

T.F.H. Publications, Inc.
One TFH Plaza
Third and Union Avenues
Neptune City, NJ 07753

Printed and bound in China

08 09 10 11 12 7 9 8 6

ISBN (revised edition): 978-0-7938-3466-2

The Library of Congress has cataloged the original edition as follows:

Anderson, Teoti.
The super simple guide to housetraining / Teoti Anderson.
p. cm.
Includes index.
ISBN 0-7938-3465-1 (alk. paper)
1. Dogs-Training. I. Title.
SF431.N528 2004
636.7'0887--dc22

                         2004004663

The Leader In Responsible Animal Care For Over 50 Years!®
www.tfh.com

Table of Contents

Part One

Introduction to Housetraining

Chapter 1

All About Housetraining

Your friends without dogs don't understand it. To them, all you talk about is pee! Today your dog peed on your expensive rug in the dining room. Last week he peed in the guest room. And then just this morning, he peed on your bed (not to mention the surprise poop he left behind the couch the other day)!

With the energy and money you've put into cleaning the messes your dog is making, your friends figure you could have paid a second mortgage by now. You've tried scolding, not scolding, rushing him out faster, leaving him out longer…but nothing seems to work!

When Fido does manage to actually eliminate outside, your friends don't understand your overwhelming joy…or the need for you to shout it from the rooftops as if you've won some sort of housetraining lottery!

You can begin housetraining your new pup as soon as you bring him home.

Okay, so they don't get it. Your friends and family may think you're a bit obsessive over your dog's elimination habits, but the truth of the matter is that it's serious business. A problem with housetraining is one of the leading reasons why people give up dogs in the US. It can often mean the real difference between Fido living happily ever after with a family or ending up in a shelter. Many people will even put up with a dog that bites them but quickly get rid of a dog that eliminates inside.

Besides, housetraining is important to you. You don't want to have to clean up your house every day. Depending on the size of the dog, cleaning up a mess can be a very big deal! It's icky and discouraging and extremely frustrating. You don't want to give up your dog; you love him. But you have to get a handle on this problem before your house turns into a sty and your family members revolt! What can you do?

HOUSETRAINING PREPARATION

You can teach a dog to eliminate outdoors. Really. The main problems with housetraining occur because we as humans communicate very differently than dogs. What you think you may be teaching your dog may not be remotely close to what he's learning. You need to communicate with him in terms he can understand, and you also need to be clear in what you're teaching him and make sure you are giving him consistent direction. This book will help you do just that.

Is it going to be easy? Not necessarily. Training a dog is hard work! You may have to do thingsthat interfere with your schedule and that take extra time out of your busy day. It would be so much easier if Fido could just read our minds! But he can't, so you'll need to carefully, clearly explain to him what you want so that he can understand your goals.

It's also going to take a lot of patience–and not just for your dog! You're going to have to learn a new way to communicate with your canine buddy. Since you're learning something new, too, you may easily become frustrated and upset when you have setbacks. But just as it's never too late to teach your dog something new, it's not too late for you, either! Have patience with yourself. You deserve a lot of credit for even trying this; there are many owners out there who would have given up on their dogs long before! Your dog is lucky to have you.

The good news is that once you get on course with a proven, successful housetraining program, you and your dog will finally be on the same page! He'll be able to live inside without turning your nice house into his private bathroom.

Super Simple Tip

To housetrain your dog, you must communicate with him in terms he can understand.

Success in housetraining depends as much on you as it does on your dog.

Housetraining is not as complicated as you might think, but it does require a great deal of patience on your part.

Now, while training your dog might be work, it doesn't have to be complicated or hard to understand. Just the opposite is true! The techniques I'll show you are super simple: They just require time, effort, and patience, especially for the first few weeks until you learn your new routine. Just look at your sweet dog's face and think back to the reason you brought him home in the first place. Isn't the extra effort worth it? Put forth the time and energy now to properly housetrain your dog, and you'll have a canine friend for life!

THE ROAD TO SUCCESSFUL HOUSETRAINING STARTS HERE

This book is a comprehensive how-to guide. It will help you chart a successful course for housetraining your dog.

- I'll cover the tools you'll need and give you tips on how to use them effectively.
- You'll learn how to set realistic expectations for your dog based on

his age and breed or combination of breeds. Yes, you can housetrain a toy dog! Even the little guys can learn to potty outside. And yes, you can train an adult dog! It's never too late to teach your dog something new.

- You'll learn how to set a new routine schedule for your dog. I'll go over a variety of options and help you come up with one that's realistic for your dog and that still fits your lifestyle.

Making the Effort

Properly housetraining your dog is not an easy task. It will take time and patience on your part to make your dog understand what you want from him and to teach him to be consistent. However, the end result—no more cleaning up after your pet's indoor "accidents"—will make all that effort worthwhile!

- You'll learn when problems may not be training-related but health-related. I'll cover nutrition and health issues that can affect your housetraining efforts. Discover what diseases and drugs can cause incontinence in dogs.
- You'll discover step-by-step instructions for crate training your dog and teaching him to potty outdoors. You'll even learn how to teach your dog to ring a bell to let you know he wants to go outside!
- I'll explain what to do if your dog has an accident and give helpful tips on cleaning up the mess so your dog doesn't go back to the same spot again and again.
- I'll also go over common challenges to housetraining so you can prevent mistakes!
- Most of all, I'll keep training fun for you and your dog. By using reward-based methods, you'll be improving your relationship with your dog while you fix his housetraining issues. Dealing with pee and poop accidents in your home every day isn't pleasant, but training your dog can be!

If you stick with the program, have patience, and are consistent, your friends and family won't have to listen to your housetraining tales of woe anymore. Instead, they'll be hearing about how smart and wonderful your dog is!

Chapter 2

What Is Housetraining?

Housetraining is teaching your dog to pee and poop only outside the house. It's pretty confusing for your dog if you want him to go outside sometimes but use newspaper or potty pads at other times. This is why the process often breaks down. It's hard for a dog to understand that sometimes it's okay to potty in the house but at other times it's not. I'll cover more about this later, as well as introduce an alternative for small breed dogs with owners who either can't or don't want them to eliminate outside. But for now, when I refer to housetraining, I mean that the dog will learn not to pee or poop inside—ever.

A truly housetrained dog never eliminates where he's not supposed to.

Some folks will say their dogs are completely housetrained…except they sometimes have accidents on the carpet. Or their dogs are completely housetrained…except their male dog occasionally lifts his leg on the entertainment center. Or their dogs are completely housetrained…except for (insert excuse here!). These dogs are, in fact, not housetrained. They have learned it's acceptable to eliminate in the house. This means that if your dog is perfectly healthy and there's no physical reason for eliminating in your house, and he is still doing it, then he's not a housetrained dog. This is nothing to be embarrassed about! You just need to admit there's a problem so you can solve it.

IT'S A NATURAL THING

All animals have to get rid of their bodies' waste—it's a natural thing they have to do. From your dog's perspective, it's probably much more pleasant to do that on the soft carpet in your climate-controlled home than outside in grass and rough weather! Dogs have all sorts of natural behaviors that we humans don't always enjoy. For example, they chew to ease their gums when they're teething, to relieve stress, because it's fun, and because they're good at it! As a result, it's a perfectly natural idea for them to chew on your furniture, your shoes, your baseball card collection, and whatever else they can get their teeth on.

Dogs also dig. They dig to make a cool hole when it's hot outside and to make a warm hole when it's cold outside. They dig looking for critters underground. They dig because it's fun, and they excel at that activity, too! It

Super Simple Tip

Be consistent when housetraining your dog. Changing his routine or your expectations too often or too quickly will only confuse him!

makes perfect sense to them, then, to dig lots of craters outdoors, making your backyard look like the surface of the moon.

Chewing, digging, eliminating: These are all natural dog behaviors. But when we bring dogs into our lives and into our households, we expect them to control their natural urges. If you think about it, we expect a lot from our dogs! We expect them to control their instincts and live by another species' rules.

Think about what it would feel like if you had to do the same. For example, have you ever met someone from a different culture? What if you were accustomed to shaking hands in greeting, but the other person considered this custom to be extremely rude? Or in some cultures, it's very normal for people of both genders to kiss strangers on the cheek in greeting. But if you weren't used to that, you might think it was a serious violation of your personal space.

It's important to understand the things that dogs do naturally so you can better understand your canine family member. This doesn't mean you have to allow those natural dog behaviors in your home. What it does mean is that it's up to you to set your expectations and make sure your dog knows what they are.

You can teach your dog to live by your rules, as long as those rules are fair and realistic. You just need to channel those behaviors into more appropriate outlets: "Please don't chew up the kids' toys. You can play with these dog-safe toys instead;" "Please don't dig pits to China in the backyard. I'm going to give you a play area where you can dig to your heart's content;" and "Please don't go potty in the house. I'd prefer you go outside."

Eliminating wastes is a normal function. Understanding this will help you better understand your dog.

Chapter 3

The Way Dogs Learn

Whenever you have any interaction with your dog, it's a good idea to ask, "What am I teaching my dog?" You may not think you're teaching your dog anything, but you probably are!

When you catch a dog in the act of peeing inside the house and you scold him, he will probably associate your scolding with his behavior. If you find the mess an hour later and then start scolding him, he will not have a clue what you're so upset about. You can point at it all you want, but your dog will just think you have a real problem with pee!

If your new pup has an accident, remember that you are just as much at fault as he is!

Remember, elimination is a natural behavior. Dogs have to do it, so it's hard for a dog to understand why you have issues with something so natural. What you actually have an issue with is where he's doing it, but your dog doesn't understand this concept. You have to teach him what you mean.

At the same time, however, physical punishment is not the answer. If you use physical punishment—a rolled-up newspaper, your hands to spank or scruff shake, etc.—to punish your dog, you may get your message across, but you are more likely to create new problems. For example, Fido poops on the rug and you catch him in the act. You race over to him and shake him, yelling that he's a bad boy. The next day, you find more poop under the dining room table. Didn't he understand you were mad at him when you punished him the day before? Yes. What he learned was that you got angry at him when he was pooping. Then you frightened him with your punishment—you taught him that you could be scary! The next day, then, he hid and pooped under the dining room table so you wouldn't catch him and scare him again.

Did you teach Fido to go outside? No. You accidentally taught him to be afraid of you. Instead of teaching him not to poop in the house, you accidentally taught him to hide when he poops. Oops! Sometimes, this lesson can cause a bigger problem…one far more serious than your already existing housetraining issue.

Let's say you catch Fido again and this time you

roll up some newspaper and swat him—not hard, but loud enough to really startle him. The next day, you catch him pooping in the house again and you reach for your newspaper. This time, Fido snarls at you! Is he being defiant? Is he being stubborn? Not at all. He's in the middle of doing something natural, something his body simply has to do, and he doesn't understand what you want. And now he's afraid, so he's going to use dog communication—in this case, a snarl—to tell you that you are scaring him and he wants you to stop.

What if you don't? What if you escalate your punishment? Maybe the newspaper wasn't enough…maybe you need to spank him to show him who's boss. If Fido thinks you are not listening to him, those snarls can become snaps, which can become bites—and all because of a misunderstanding. Now, in addition to a housetraining problem, you've got an aggression problem!

Never punish your dog for having an accident—he'll only learn to mistrust and fear you.

Unfortunately, this is a common mistake people make when trying to communicate with their dogs. Remember, aggression begets aggression. When you use aggressive tactics with your dog, you're teaching him that's how to solve a problem. And you don't want your dog to think that's the way to do anything! It's like teaching a human child to solve disagreements with a punch. You don't have to follow that path. There's a super simple way to teach your dog to eliminate outside, without having to resort to old-fashioned physical discipline. It's effective and less stressful for both of you!

Part Two

Getting Ready

Chapter 4

Before You Begin

Before you take a trip, you make sure you've packed everything and know exactly where you're going, right? If you forget something, you may experience some frustration, and your trip may not be as pleasant as you had hoped.

Just like a trip, before you start training it's important to make sure you have everything ready and you understand the route you're going to take. How long should your dog be able to "hold it?" Is it really harder to housetrain one breed versus another? What kind of equipment do you need? How long is this trip going to take, anyway? Good preparation will set you up for success…so let's start!

Super Simple Tip

Not every dog will become housetrained the same way or in the same amount of time. Try to establish a housetraining regimen that's ideal for your individual pet.

Make sure you know and understand your dog well before you begin training him.

KNOWING YOUR DOG

Every dog is different. There are lots of factors that will determine how long your dog should be able to go without needing a potty break. The better you understand your dog, the better you'll be able to housetrain him!

Age

How old is your dog? Age plays an important factor in how long your dog can wait in between potty breaks and if he's able to understand what you're trying to teach him.

5–7 Weeks

At this stage, puppies start learning how to act like dogs. The mother dog may begin weaning puppies around the fourth week. She also teaches discipline and they begin to learn bite inhibition (not to bite down too hard on their littermates). This is a very important time in a puppy's development; he will learn many social skills from his

Early Lessons Are Important

Given the option, most puppies don't want to eliminate near where they eat. But what about the puppies that have no choice? If your puppy was raised in a cage or a small kennel, he had no choice. He had to eliminate in his den because that's the only place he could. This means that he was surrounded by his own waste at an impressionable age and will most likely continue this same behavior in the future.

If he was taken from his mother too early, he also missed out on another important lesson—mother dogs lick their puppies after they eliminate so that they learn to be clean. If your pup was removed from his mother too early, no one taught him how to be clean. As a result, he may think it's acceptable to be messy, to step in his poop, and to have it all over his body.

It's important to remember that it's not your puppy's fault if he was raised this way. Anyone who breeds puppies should know better; the sad fact is, though, that not all of them care to do it right. And if you didn't know not to buy a puppy raised like this, it's not your fault, either—now you do know better, so you won't make the same mistake again! Unfortunately, the consequences are that you now have a puppy that thinks it's fine to eliminate wherever he is, and living in his own waste doesn't bug him in the least.

Consequently, you will face a greater housetraining challenge with this puppy. You can housetrain him, but be advised that it will take much more patience and consistency on your part because you have to make up for those who taught him wrong in the first place.

littermates that will help him deal with humans and other dogs later in life.

If puppies are removed from their litters during this time, they may have trouble becoming good pets, and it can be harder to teach them to play nicely with those teeth!

If puppies are properly housed at this crucial stage, they will learn the beginning concepts of housetraining. Puppies that have a choice will usually leave the place where they eat and eliminate somewhere else, even if it's just to wobble across to the other side of the whelping box. If they are unable to do this, then they may learn that it's okay to eliminate in their dens.

Your dog will have learned many of his housetraining instincts from his mother and litter-mates.

8–16 Weeks

This is a critically important time in your puppy's life: It's a short window where your puppy learns that the world is a wonderful place or a terrifying one. If your puppy doesn't meet lots of people and other dogs at this time, he may develop fear or aggression problems later.

If housetraining is inconsistent or scary now, it may cause your puppy to have problems with housetraining later, too.

Sometimes during this period, puppies appear to be completely housetrained. Some will even go towards the door when they have to eliminate, but this is where mistakes in housetraining and unrealistic expectations will come back to haunt you. Puppies may sometimes seem to understand the concept and then the next day will piddle all over your carpet. This is because they are still babies and are just learning bladder control.

At eight weeks of age, puppies can usually wait about two hours before needing a potty break. At 16 weeks, they can hold it for four hours or so. Some owners make the mistake of pushing this limit, which could lead to problems. Your puppy will either have an accident because he can't hold it any longer, or if he does manage to hold it, he could contract a urinary tract infection if it's been too long a wait.

4–6 Months

If you thought your puppy was housetrained before, he could prove you wrong now. At this age, he's so easily distracted you think he'll never focus on anything. In fact, just when you think he's about to potty outside, he'll chase a butterfly! This is normal. He's exploring his world! Puppies that are four months old can go about four to five hours without a potty break. At six months, your puppy should be able to go about six or seven hours.

Distractions while housetraining your pup will make it more difficult for him to learn his lesson.

What Makes a Dog Easy to Housetrain?

Age isn't the only thing that affects a dog's response to housetraining. How well your pet will take to training also depends on several other factors, including gender, the breed of the dog, and any past training he may have.

6–12 Months

Puppies start developing sexually. You may notice behaviors in your unneutered male you never noticed before, including raising his leg and peeing on your furniture! Your female can have her first heat anywhere from 6 to 12 months of age.

If your puppy has had a good, consistent housetraining program up to this time, he should be able to go about seven to eight hours in between potty breaks. This is when people often make the mistake of thinking their puppies are fully housetrained, so they let them have the run of the house when they're out, only to find accidents when they return home.

Puppies may not associate their dens with your entire house until they're a year old. Basically, it all depends on the puppy and how he's been trained.

12–24 Months

A puppy's breed and size will determine maturity. Small dogs are usually considered adults at about one year of age, while larger dogs take two full years to grow into adulthood. Some giant breeds take even longer!

Adult Dogs

If your puppy has had irregular housetraining up until this point, he may be pretty confused about where to eliminate. Maybe you even adopted an older dog and have no idea what his early learning and training experience were like. Adult dogs can learn housetraining. Just because a dog is fully mature doesn't mean his brain stops working. You can housetrain an older dog with super simple methods, too! It's never too late for dogs—and humans—to learn something new. You just may have to have some extra patience while you make up for some misguided early lessons. Rest assured that your patience and consistency will pay off!

Gender

Male dogs can be harder to housetrain than female dogs. When males become sexually mature, they may start lifting their legs and peeing to mark territory in the house. Neutering your dog at an early age at your veterinarian's recommendation will often prevent this problem from ever starting in the first place. But what if you already have to deal with this issue? Well, the longer it's been going on, the harder it will be to fix.

This is simply because your dog has had a longer time to practice the habit! The habit itself begins due to the influence of hormones—your dog wants to mark his territory. However, the more often he does it, the more of a habit it becomes. That's why if you neuter your dog later in life, after he's been marking indoor territory for years, he won't magically stop peeing on your entertainment center. Even if the problem has been going on for a while, though, you can still housetrain your dog; it will just take more persistence on your part.

It may be tempting to try and classify this as a male dominance problem or a hormonal issue, but when you're trying to change dog behavior, cut through the clutter. What's the real issue in this case? Your dog is peeing in your house. It doesn't matter why your dog is doing it, you just don't want him to continue!

If your puppy had irregular housetraining up until adulthood, he may be confused as to what you expect of him now.

Smaller breeds need to be taken out more often. Make sure you can recognize all the signs that your dog needs to eliminate.

Thus, it's really a housetraining issue. You want your dog to eliminate outside instead of inside. This guide will help your male dog keep his marking outside where it belongs, instead of all over your furniture.

Breed

Yes, it's harder to housetrain toy breeds than larger ones. This could be because toy breeds are so tiny that their digestive systems process everything quickly, making them eliminate more often. It could also be because when they do have accidents, toy breeds are so quick that it's very hard to catch them in the act. A week could go by before you even noticed an accident!

Housetraining might also be more difficult for smaller dogs because people tend to coddle toy dogs more and accept worse behavior. For example, some owners think it's hilarious when their Chihuahua growls at people, while a Rottweiler's owner would be very concerned. If you set low expectations for a dog, then that's all he'll ever meet! So when a toy breed piddles on the carpet, it's considered to be an annoying yet small problem; yet when a Great Dane does it, the owner takes quick action because there's a much bigger mess!

In short, it may take you longer to housetrain a toy breed dog, but little dogs can learn to eliminate outside just like the big boys! (After all, they do think they're big dogs, don't they?)

Past Training

Some folks try all kinds of different methods in a desperate attempt to train their dogs to eliminate outside. This will just confuse your dog even more! If you tried paper training for two weeks, then wee-wee pads for another couple of weeks, then bought a crate, then got rid of the crate because your pup whined in it, then went back to the paper, how do you think your dog supposed to keep up? He can't.

If you're not consistent with your training methods, your dog is not going to have a clue as to what you want him to do. He may never become 100-percent housetrained at this rate because the rules keep changing. Dogs are very much creatures of routine; they like their worlds to be predictable, a factor that will actually help you housetrain your dog.

First, a consistent plan needs to be established to get you both back on track. Once you start following a successful plan, it's much easier for your dog to understand what you want. It may be shaky at first because your dog is expecting you to change your mind again! However, stick with the plan and you'll see success!

Be consistent with your housetraining methods.

Chapter 5

The Right Equipment

You're going to need some basic equipment for your new housetraining regimen to be successful. Have the right tools on hand and it'll make your job that much easier!

Dogs that are not housetrained and that have the run of the house will eliminate all over the place. They have no concept that the vast space they're running around in should not be their personal toilet. An effective housetraining program begins with confinement.

You need to limit the dog's space because most animals do not want to eliminate in their dens. As they learn bladder and bowel control, you can increase their amount of freedom so they gradually understand your entire house is off limits for elimination.

A DOG'S DEN: HIS CRATE

One of the best ways to safely and effectively confine your dog is with a crate. A crate is basically a box. No, it's not a jail or a prison, but rather a kind of doggie playpen. Crates come in a variety of materials: some are plastic, wire, epoxy-covered wire, canvas, and even stylish rattan! There are different styles, colors, and features, but they all share one basic concept—a crate is your dog's private, safe den.

Some folks have a hard time with the entire crate concept, and it can be a little unnerving if you think like a human. However, remember that dogs are den animals. They often wedge themselves into unlikely spaces and curl up for a good nap. Have you ever found your dog happily curled up underneath the coffee table? They don't mind confinement, as long as it's used as one part of your overall training program, and you balance it with proper exercise and plenty of quality time outside the crate.

What if you confined your dog in a small room instead of using a crate? Some dogs do absolutely fine with this method, but the following

You need the right equipment to properly train your dog.

You can make your dog's crate more comfortable by adding some safe chew toys.

are some risks to consider:

1. Dogs left in the kitchen or bathroom can still access things that can hurt them. One day your puppy will be a little angel; the next day, all your cabinets will be rounded off when you get home! Sure, this is a major inconvenience and it's bound to make you angry…but it's also dangerous. Dogs can get splinters in their gums from wood, experience stomach blockages from eating toilet paper, or generally hurt themselves from chewing on something that isn't good for them. If a dog is in a crate, he can't get hold of dangerous items in the first place.

2. Dogs often escape from confinement to a room. They may learn to jump over the baby gate, or even hit it in just the right place to pop it loose from the doorway. Then they have the rest of your house as a playground! This is just giving them a chance to practice behavior you don't want—or an opportunity to get into something else that can hurt them.

    Keeping your pet behind closed doors doesn't always work, either. I knew one determined dog that chewed his way through a bathroom door! He didn't make it all the way through, but his owners were less than thrilled to see his smiling face poking through the gaping hole in their door. Other dogs will just scratch and paw a doorway to ribbons, adding home repair bills to your cleaning costs. Crates are much more secure.

3. If the room is too big, your puppy may still have plenty of room to pee or poop in a corner and stay high and dry the rest of the time you're gone. In fact, a large room will teach your dog it's okay to eliminate in the house, which is the exact opposite of what you want!

Learning to Love the Crate

A properly crate-trained dog doesn't see his crate as a prison or a place he's sent to for punishment. Never put your dog in his crate if he has an accident or does something wrong, or he will never learn to appreciate the crate for the comfortable retreat it can (and should!) be.

6 Reasons Crates Are Great

It's true that just like with any tool, a crate can be abused. For example, it would be cruel to leave your puppy in a crate for 20 hours. It's very important to give your dog the proper exercise for his age and breed (or mix of breeds!) and quality attention and affection time outside of a crate. However, properly introducing a crate may be one of the best things you do for your dog, even without considering the fact that it'll help you tremendously with housetraining. The following are some reasons why:

1. If your dog is safely in his crate when you can't supervise him, he can't chew or eat something that will hurt him. You'll also have to replace fewer shoes, underwear, your kids' toys, magazines, etc.

2. If you have workers over at your house hooking up the cable or fixing the dishwasher, a crate keeps your dog safe and out from underfoot!

3. Ever have visitors to your home who are afraid of dogs? Maybe a small toddler your dog could easily knock over, or a fragile senior who won't appreciate your exuberant dog leaping into his or her lap? If your dog is in his crate, your friends can enjoy a peaceful visit. (You can later use that opportunity to train your dog to have some nice manners for visiting company!)

4. Do you want to travel with your dog? Hotels love a dog that is crate trained because it ensures their rooms will be in good condition when you leave. Despite your best efforts to put up the "Do Not

If you travel with your dog, his crate will be a familiar place where he feels safe.

Disturb" sign when you leave for breakfast, there's a chance the hotel maids may ignore it and walk right into your room. If your dog is loose, he could escape! Too many dogs have escaped from hotel rooms and were never seen again.

If you travel with your dog, bring a crate. It will also help when you get to your destination. Visiting a strange place can be stressful for a dog, but he'll feel very comfortable in his familiar, safe den that you brought along.

5. Hopefully, your dog will never have to spend the night at the veterinarian's, but if he does, your veterinarian will not let him have the run of the clinic overnight! He's going to put Fido in a kennel or a cage, and it's much better for your dog if he's already used to being confined. If not, your dog could become very stressed and hurt himself trying to get out. The same goes for any groomer visits. When your dog is not getting the spa treatment, he's going to be in a crate or kennel. It's much less stressful for the

dog if he's used to the idea.

Crates also come in handy for health reasons. There may be times when your veterinarian asks you to confine your dog, maybe due to an injury or infection. Let's say your dog leaps out of the car and twists his leg, and the vet tells you your dog must completely rest that leg for two weeks. You observe your dog boinging off the walls and wonder how you're going to prevent him from zooming off the furniture, let alone walking on his injured leg. A crate provides the perfect solution.

6. The safest place for your dog in a car is in his crate. Dogs should never be allowed to run loose in a car. They can easily cause an accident by getting tangled up in your lap or your car's controls. They are also most easily injured in an accident if you have to slam on the brakes or if someone cuts you off in traffic.

Dogs become projectiles in accidents. They can go right through a windshield or get thrown about in your car. If your dog runs off after an accident and you're injured and unable to speak, the

Bringing the Outside Dog Inside

If you purchased this book, you probably have a dog that lives inside most of the time. However, maybe you have an outside dog and would really like him to live in the house with you. Good for you! Dogs are pack animals, and they can develop behavior problems if they live outside and only get to see people a couple of times a day. They can be harder to train because they're not as closely bonded with humans as dogs that live inside with their families. A dog that has the best outdoor situation—great shelter, plenty of water and food— would still have a better quality of life indoors because, on an emotional level, they need to be with their people.

Of course, you may be worried. If your dog has only lived outside, you don't want him trashing your house! Maybe you have a spouse who isn't too keen on bringing Rover into the homestead. A crate can help ease your transition.

Train your outside dog to love his crate, and you'll have a nice, safe den to keep him indoors when you can't supervise him. You'll also be working on your housetraining with the crate. You can even start teaching him some family manners using reward-based methods. Best of all, your family will rest assured that you're working to bring Rover into the house with a plan for success!

The crate is rather like a doggie playpen.

folks who come to rescue you may not even know there was a dog in the car! There have also been cases in which dogs have tried to protect their owners who were injured in a car accident. Medical personnel are on the scene to help you first and foremost. If your dog is going to pose a danger to them, they may have to make the difficult decision to hurt your dog in order to get to you, which will delay your medical care.

Please keep your dog safe. Get a crate and secure it in your backseat, because front airbags can severely injure or kill your dog if deployed. If your car is too small to hold a crate, then buy a dog seatbelt and secure your dog in the backseat.

Finding the Right Crate

These are just some of the many reasons why crate training is a good thing, but how do you decide what crate to buy? How do you choose with so many different styles? Here are a few tips:

1. For housetraining purposes, your dog should just be able to stand up, stretch out, and turn around in his crate. Anything bigger and he will still be able to eliminate in his crate and stay high

and dry the rest of the time, which will make it harder for him to learn bladder and bowel control. Buying a small crate may seem especially cruel at first, but I'll explain how your dog will gradually earn more privileges—including space—the more he learns what you want!

2. Do you have a medium or large breed puppy? You may not want to buy a crate for every stage of your dog's development. It could end up being quite expensive, depending on how big your puppy grows. Blocking the back of a large crate with a box or something to make it smaller may just provide your puppy with a bad chew toy! Instead, try getting a crate that comes with a convenient, sturdy divider. You can then move the divider as the puppy matures, so the crate will grow with your puppy!

3. Do you want a crate that you can put away when you need the extra room? Or do you want one that can be conveniently moved

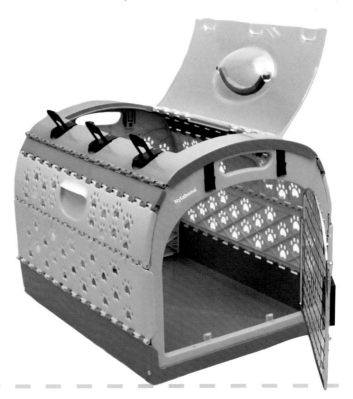

Folding crates set up easily and can be stored away when not in use.

into different rooms of your home? Get a crate that folds up like a suitcase, such as those made by Nylabone. Folding crates even come with handles so you can carry them easily. These are perfect if you want to buy only one crate and let your puppy spend his days in the living room and nights in your bedroom. You can just fold the crate up and move it! They're also convenient for traveling. Furthermore, your

Canvas crates are suitable for small, crate-trained dogs when traveling.

puppy may not need to be crated forever, so when your dog is fully housetrained, you can just fold up the crate and save it for your next canine family member!

4. Should you purchase a plastic or wire crate? It's really a matter of personal preference. Plastic crates are very sturdy—they come apart for easy cleaning and storage. They also come in a variety of colors, although with some brands, the color depends on the size of the crate. For example, the large size crate may only come in beige, while the small crate may only come in blue. Plastic crates may somewhat obstruct your dog's view of the environment. For this reason, if you have a very reactive dog—one that barks whenever he sees something—you may want to try a plastic crate. Some dogs do like to chew on the plastic, leaving rough edges. Plastic crates are also approved for airline travel, and some even come with wheels so you can easily roll them along. Please check with each individual airline to make sure you understand their regulations for canine travel.

Wire crates usually fold up for easy storage and travel. They have sturdy plastic or metal pans in the bottom to catch messes, and the pans easily slide out for cleaning. Epoxy-coated versions are resistant to rust. Wire crates are very good for chewers—it's harder for a dog to damage a wire crate. They usually come in gold, white, or black, and you normally get to choose the color you want in the size you want. However, make sure you choose one with small holes—you don't want your dog to get his paw caught. Wire crates also offer your dog a better view because there are openings all

A Crate Built for Two

Some folks get littermates or two young puppies and want to keep them together in a large crate. There are advantages and disadvantages to this.

Advantages:
- You only have to buy one crate.
- The puppies can entertain each other when they're in the crate.
- You may feel less guilty leaving them in the crate if they have each other for company.

Disadvantages:
- You'll need to buy a large enough crate to accommodate two growing puppies, so it may also end up being big enough where they can still feel comfortable enough to eliminate in the crate. This will undo your housetraining efforts.
- Your puppies may become overly dependent on each other. Puppies that spend all their time with another puppy grow more bonded to that puppy than their human families. At first, they may seem like ideal babysitters for each other, but you will soon realize that neither one pays you much attention! If they ever have to be separated—for example, if one puppy ever has to visit the veterinarian alone—the puppy left behind could be traumatized because he's not used to being alone without his canine pal.
- As your puppies get older, they could start squabbling. How would you like to be stuck in a crate with a pesky sibling all the time? If one puppy is having a bad day or just wants to be left alone, there's nowhere to go for solo time.

Whatever you decide, it's important you separate the puppies often and spend quality time with them as individuals so they learn to bond with you. It's also important to train them individually—it's too hard to train two bouncy puppies at once! Once they learn what you want and are performing well as singles, then you can combine them for training.

around. If you want your dog to have a better view of his environment, you may prefer a wire crate.

5. Do you have a chewer, or maybe a puppy that's still teething? How about an adult dog that's destructive? Stick to the strong wire or plastic crates. Canvas crates are wonderful for traveling, but they make expensive chew toys! Canvas or lightweight travel crates are best for dogs that are completely crate trained and that won't chew their crates or eliminate in them. If your dog is not completely crate trained, then don't buy a lightweight travel crate.

Wire crates are very good for dogs who like to chew.

One final thing I'd like to mention is the luggage-type carrier. They look just like an overnight suitcase or makeup bag, with a shoulder strap. These are great for traveling with small dogs and cats, but they are not ideal for housetraining because they are harder to clean.

With so many people buying crates for their dogs, companies are trying harder to make them more attractive for today's designer homes. Some crates, like ones made of rattan, can be attractive additions to your home. But these crates are also best for dogs that are already completely crate trained. If you want to jazz up your dog's crate, some companies make designer covers and crate beds that will fit right in with your décor. Again, make sure your puppy won't pull a crate cover through a wire crate wall and chew it to bits!

You can still find attractive crates in wire or plastic. I'll teach you how to properly crate train your dog, so if you want him to graduate to a designer crate, you'll know how to get there!

Where do you get the perfect crate? You can find them at your local pet store, some discount price warehouses, discount department stores, mail order catalogs, and of course, online. Shop around—you'll find the prices do vary!

Once you feel that your dog is house-trained, you can use a baby gate to limit his access to certain areas of the house.

Where to Place Your Crate

Once you get your crate, where do you set it up? It should be where your family is. Dogs are pack animals. Your dog loves you and wants to be with you! If a dog is kept isolated from the family, he won't learn to bond with his family. He can also develop behavioral problems later.

It's up to you whether you want the crate to be in your bedroom at night. Some folks want their dogs to sleep with them, and others don't. Generally, your dog will prefer to be where you are, but if you don't want your dog's crate in the bedroom, he will survive just fine.

What's confusing to a dog is when you can't make up your mind—you start in the bedroom for a couple of weeks, then kick him out for a while, then let him back in. Just decide what you want and be consistent. You'll both learn a routine a lot faster that way!

LIMITING SPACE: BABY GATES

Crate training is extremely effective in housetraining your dog, but as your dog better understands what you want, you are going to have to gradually increase the amount of space your dog has access to. For some folks, it's easy to remember to shut doors to block off certain rooms. But do you have people in your house who can't remember where they put their shoes, let alone remember to shut a door? If not, don't be discouraged. Every family has them! Unfortunately, though, these loveable but forgetful folks can undo your training efforts!

Save yourself some aggravation and training setbacks by investing in a couple of baby gates. You can get these at baby stores or pet supply stores. There are a few varieties to choose from: Some are permanent (they come with hardware you use to install them into your doorframe), while others are more easily moved from door to door. If the thought of stepping over baby gates is already giving you a leg cramp, get the kind that has a swing door built right into the gate for easy access for you and your family members.

USING BELLYBANDS

Do you have an unneutered male dog that already has the habit of marking in your home? Do you perhaps own a toy breed male that's so lightning fast when he pees indoors you just can't catch him in the act? Maybe you adopted a retired racing Greyhound that's still learning what it's like to live indoors, and he's been peeing on your carpet. If any of these scenarios sound familiar, you may want to consider getting some bellybands to help you with your housetraining.

Bellybands are strips of fabric with Velcro on the ends. You insert a feminine pad inside them and then wrap the cloth around your dog's lower belly. If he raises his leg to pee indoors, he'll just pee on the pad, not on your furniture.

You can find bellybands at some pet stores and at online retailers. They come in a variety of fabrics, so you can indulge your fashion sense while you housetrain your boy! They're machine-washable, and you just replace the feminine pads as needed.

Bellybands alone will not housetrain your dog. You'll still need to follow a housetraining program if you want to teach your dog to eliminate outdoors, but they can be a useful tool to help you reach your goal.

GETTING ATTACHED: LEASHES AND COLLARS

When you start your housetraining program and take your dogs outside to eliminate, it's important you're attached to them. If you're not attached to your dog, you can't control the environment. Of course, a dog should never be loose in an unfenced area—the risk of danger is just too great! Even if you have a fenced-in yard, though, you're setting yourself up for failure if you let your puppy off leash when you're trying

Other Collar Choices

Head halters are growing in popularity and are a humane, effective tool for working with your dog. Head halters for dogs work the same as halters for horses—control the head, control the animal! Make sure you get the right size for your dog, and get a professional to fit it properly and show you how to use it. If you have a dog that pulls badly or jumps up on people a lot, a head halter is a good choice to help give you more control. Although they used to be mistaken for muzzles, head halters couldn't be more different. Your dog is free to take treats and give kisses, unlike with a muzzle. And they come in a variety of cool colors, so you can indulge your creative side!

Limited slip or martingale collars are good for dogs with slender necks and those that could easily wiggle out of a regular collar, like Greyhounds or Dobermans. These are not to be mistaken for slip collars or choke chains, as there is a limit to the amount of tension you can apply on the collar. Some martingale collars are quite elaborate and would please the pickiest of fashion designers, while some are just simple and practical.

Harnesses are popular, especially with owners of smaller dogs. Some dogs have trachea problems, and a veterinarian may have recommended a harness instead of a regular collar. Sometimes, dogs pull so much they sound like they're choking all the time, so an owner may try a harness to prevent his or her dog from passing out. When properly fitted, harnesses are fine for training, although there is a consequence to using them.

Basically, harnesses more effectively distribute weight across a dog's body, making it easier for a dog to pull. Just think of the device used to hook Huskies up to sleds. If you're more comfortable using a harness on your dog, that's fine…just be aware that when you're training your dog to walk politely on leash, you may have a slightly greater challenge.

to housetrain him.

Puppies chase butterflies. They roll in smelly things. They tackle leaves and do battle with pinecones. In short, they have no attention span whatsoever. Even your older dog may have trouble staying focused. Remember, your dog doesn't have a clue what you want him to do! You haven't taught him yet.

If your dog is not attached to you, you're giving him the chance to become distracted. This means that instead of remembering he has to pee, he'll perk up at the ice cream man's jingle and dash off for the fence gate, barking madly. Instead of finding the perfect spot to poop, he'll bounce over to give kisses to your neighbor's kids as they hang over the fence. Save yourself a lot of wasted time chasing Fido all over the yard. Leash him!

There's another benefit to teaching your dog to potty on leash. Imagine you're on a road trip and you've brought your best canine friend with you. You've got a long road ahead, so you take a few rest stops. It's certainly not safe to let your dog just run loose, so you take him out on leash and wait for him to go. Instead, he looks at you like you're crazy, following him around!

Many dogs that are never trained to potty on leash get stressed and nervous when you follow them around. They won't go! They then end up holding it too long, which can make them sick. However, if you've trained

Your dog should always wear his collar and leash when outside.

your dog to potty on leash, this won't be a problem! Use a 4- to 6-foot (1- to 2-m) leash, one that feels comfortable to you. It can be nylon, cotton, leather, or whatever you choose. If you have a toy breed dog, make sure the metal snap is not too heavy.

I don't recommend using retractable leashes for training, as they teach your dog to have a constant tension on his collar. Retractable leashes can teach your dog to pull! Ideally, you want your dog to learn there should be slack in the collar, not constant tension. Retractable leashes are great for later, when your dog has learned family manners and not to pull on leash, so save them for when your dog is already trained.

Speaking of collars, what kind should you use? There are tons of collars on the market. I recommend a plain, flat buckle, or quick-snap collar. As a reward-based trainer, I don't use choke chains or prong collars to train dogs—they're just not necessary. Those collars use the principle of physical punishment to train, and I don't find it necessary or effective to use physical punishment when training dogs. A regular flat collar will work just fine.

CLEANUP ON AISLE TWO: CLEANSERS

Despite your best efforts, there are going to be times when your dog has an accident in the house. There may already have been many of those times, which is why you're clutching this book! One of the secrets to prevent your dog from repeating that performance is a good cleanser.

Vinegar doesn't cut it. Your average name-brand carpet cleaner doesn't cut it. And forget the name-brand disinfectant cleaners, too. Oh, they all do a good job of cleaning…it's just not good enough for your dog.

Your dog's nose is a powerful instrument. People train dogs to sniff out drugs, bombs, termites, and even cancer! You may think after using a cleanser that your house smells like springtime potpourri, but your dog can smell through the flowers right into the urine lurking below. And if your dog can smell a spot where he has eliminated previously, he'll likely go there again. It's been "marked" for him to repeat the behavior.

If your dog has an accident in the house, make sure you use a pet-specific cleanser. There are some very effective ones on the market that have enzymes in them that are specifically formulated to clean up pet messes. You can find pet enzymatic cleansers in pet stores, some

Your dog has a strong sense of smell, which is why it's so important to use the right cleanser when cleaning up an accident.

discount department stores, through online retailers, and even from your veterinarian or groomer. There are some other powerful cleansers that you won't find in stores but are only available from your veterinarian's office. You may pay a bit more for these cleansers, but the effective ones are well worth the price! Your home will smell fresh and clean, and your dog will be much less likely to eliminate in the same spot over and over again.

IF YOUR DOG SIMPLY HAS TO GO INSIDE: THE LITTER BOX

As I've mentioned, I don't personally recommend using indoor housetraining methods. If you teach your dog it's okay to pee or poop inside your house, it will be hard for him to understand to only go on newspaper or on potty or "wee wee" pads. In fact, he may actually be learning to go inside the house, period.

Your dog can't possibly know the difference between eliminating on the newspaper you've already read and the edition you haven't. This means that if you're curled up on the floor with a cup of coffee and the

The Nose Knows

Your dog's sense of smell is incredibly strong, which is why using the right kind of cleanser is crucial when cleaning up an accident. If even the slightest hint of a smell remains (which may be true even if you no longer smell anything), your dog is much more likely to eliminate in the same spot in your home. Make sure to use a product that completely eliminates odors, such as the enzymatic cleansers available in pet stores and other retailers.

Sunday paper, you can't get mad at your dog if he comes and pees on your sports page!

Your dog is also very likely to use potty pads as chew toys—they shred quite nicely! And even if he gets the concept, if you later change your mind and want him to go outside, it will be hard for him to understand you changed the rules. It's much easier for your dog to learn the concept of only eliminating outside your home.

What if you live in a high-rise apartment and it's hard to take your small breed dog outside, especially in bad weather? What if you've exhausted every option and you just can't get someone to check on your young puppy during the day when you're at work? If you have a toy or small breed dog, there is an indoor housetraining method that is easier for your dog to understand—use a litter box. Litter boxes do offer some distinct advantages over other methods, such as newspapers or potty pads.

1. A litter box is a unique, predefined area. There's no chance of you having litter boxes strewn about the house that may confuse your puppy about where to eliminate.
2. Although some puppies will chew on anything, they can't tear a litter box or shake it and "kill" it, which lessens its appeal as a chew toy.
3. A litter box is easy to maintain and keep clean, so it's much more hygienic than having waste on your floor.

Granted, a litter box is not the solution for a large breed dog. Can you imagine the size of the litter box you'd need for a Mastiff? This is why I still maintain that a true housetraining regimen with the goal of outdoor elimination is best for medium-sized and larger dogs. However, if you have a toy or small-breed dog and you really want him to eliminate inside, choose a method that will be easiest for your dog to understand—the litter box.

First, buy one that will be large enough for your puppy as he grows. There is dog litter on the market. If you can't find it in your area, consult your veterinarian about what kind of litter would be safe for your puppy. Remember, puppies will often eat things that cats wouldn't, so you want to make sure any litter you use will not harm him if he decides to snack on it. If you have cats, make sure your puppy has his own litter box; you will train him to use his and his alone. If you let your puppy use your cat's litter box, your cat may stop using it altogether. Instead, your cat might find a delightful place to potty instead, like your shoes. Then you will have more than one housetraining problem on your hands!

If you choose the litter box method, you must clean it every day. More than once a day is great, but once a day at the very least. You can't let waste accumulate in the litter box, or your puppy will not want to eliminate there. In addition, it's not healthy for the waste to sit there for long periods of time. Clean your litter box at least once a day, and your house will smell much better, too. After all, just because you know you have a litter box doesn't mean you want all your houseguests to know, too!

You will train your puppy to use the litter box very similarly to how you'll train him to go outside.

Depending on the circumstances, small-breed dogs may do well with a litter box.

Part Three

Healthy Dog, Healthy Habits

Chapter 6

Proper Nutrition

You've heard it before—you are what you eat. Well, what you feed your puppy shapes his future self, too. If we ate junk food all the time, it would eventually catch up to us. We'd lose our stamina, put on the pounds, and develop health problems. It would be hard for us to concentrate and listen to what people were telling us. We'd get tired easily, our digestive systems would rebel, and we'd develop stomach problems. Sure, junk food might be tasty and okay for an occasional treat, but a diet of pure junk food would be a really bad choice over the course of a lifetime!

Dogs need good nutrition, just like we do. If you feed your puppy quality food, then your puppy's body will be healthier. And a healthy body also means a healthy mind!

IT'S IN THE BAG...OR IS IT?

The more you learn about dog nutrition, the more you'll realize that all dog food is not alike. Read the labels and find out what the ingredients exactly mean. You may be surprised at what you find! For example, there's a big difference between "chicken" on a dog food label and "chicken byproducts." Byproducts can be beaks, legs, and other chicken parts. Is that really what you want to feed your dog? Some dog foods also contain a lot of sweeteners to make them more appealing, but do you want to be feeding Fido all that sugar? No wonder he's bouncing off the walls!

Some dogs have special needs that require special diets. If your dog is allergic to a certain ingredient, for example, your veterinarian may recommend a specific brand or type of food.

You may have to pay more for a quality dog food, but it'll save you money in the long run. Quality food translates into a healthy coat, clear eyes and ears, strong muscles, a happy dog, and fewer veterinarian visits due to poor nutrition! Your dog will also have less waste because his body will absorb those good nutrients instead of passing bulk he doesn't need through his system.

If you are feeding your dog a quality food, please don't add anything to it without checking with your veterinarian. The simple act of adding some yogurt to your dog's food bowl to aid in digestion may throw off calcium levels. Plopping a raw egg in there for a shiny coat may throw off protein levels. If you mess with these nutrients, you could affect the way your dog grows. Some puppies, especially large breed dogs, are very sensitive to levels of certain nutrients, so instead of helping them be healthier, you could be creating serious health problems. Make sure you only supplement your dog's diet with your veterinarian's approval.

HOME COOKIN' AND RAW DIETS

Using people food as treats for training is fine in moderation, but it's not a good idea to share your home-cooked meals with your dog as his daily source of nutrition. What may be nutritional for you may not be the right combination of nutrients for your dog. Remember, they're a different species!

Different-sized breeds need different things. For example, if you have too much protein or calcium in your German Shepherd puppy's diet, you could cause growth problems. That leftover bacon you had for breakfast may make your Chihuahua drool, but tiny dogs should not have too much sodium in their diets. It's important to remember that just because your dog may love your leftovers doesn't mean they're a healthy choice. Do your dog a favor and save your home cookin' for the humans in your family!

Proper nutrition keeps your dog happy and healthy, which makes housetraining easier.

There is a popular trend toward feeding dogs raw diets. A raw diet consists mainly of uncooked meat and vegetables. Fans of raw diets say their dogs' coats are glossy, teeth shiny and free of tartar, and their pets experience fewer diseases. Some people make raw food meals themselves, but there are an increasing number of companies that specialize in raw diets for busy folks who would rather place an order than spend time in the kitchen!

If you want to explore feeding raw bones and food to your dog, please do your research first! Consult a veterinarian experienced

Make sure the food you offer your dog meets his nutritional requirements.

in raw diets, and get several books on the subject to help you formulate the right food for your dog.

WHICH FOOD IS RIGHT FOR YOUR DOG?

Choosing dog foods is a hot debate. It's important that you do your research to find out what food is right for your particular dog. Consult your veterinarian and your dog's breeder. Some dog magazines, like the *Whole Dog Journal*, research different dog foods and rate them on a regular basis. You should also read labels and find out what nutrition your dog needs and what foods best match those requirements.

Whatever food you choose for your dog, always keep an eye on his health to make sure you're on the right culinary path. Your dog should have firm stools, and he shouldn't strain to eliminate. If he has diarrhea or vomiting, check with your veterinarian. Some food can also contribute to skin problems. Check your dog's skin regularly—if it's dry with flaky dandruff, or if it's red and itchy, it's time to give your veterinarian a call!

Your dog doesn't get to choose from a menu or visit any restaurant he wants. He depends on you to feed him quality, nutritious meals. If you do your research, you'll be helping him live a long and healthy life!

HOW OFTEN SHOULD YOU FEED YOUR DOG?

I do not recommend free-feeding your dog, which is the practice of leaving the food bowl out all day and just filling it up as Fido eats it. Free-feeding can lead to digestive problems and obesity. If you have more than one family member in your household, it can also be hard to keep track of who filled up the food bowl last. Your dog can get pretty good at fooling folks into thinking he hasn't eaten all day!

Some dog owners opt to prepare their own meals rather than use a commercial dog food.

Food that goes in a dog on schedule comes out of a dog on schedule. It's easy on your dog's digestive system and makes it much easier to housetrain your dog. If you feed your dog all day, then your dog will have to poop all day. But if you feed your dog at regularly scheduled times, your dog's body will only have to poop at certain times. Check with your veterinarian, but the general practice is to feed dogs six months and younger three set meals a day, and older dogs twice a day.

What if you've been free-feeding your dog and he's already used to it? Your dog can learn a new schedule; you just have to be consistent. Fill the dog's food bowl and put it down for 10 minutes or so. If he eats it all, great! If not, then just take up whatever's left and try again at the next designated mealtime. Your dog is smart! He won't starve himself and will soon learn there is a limited window for his meals.

Making the Switch

If you plan to switch your dog from commercial foods to a raw diet (or vice versa), discuss the switch with your vet and proceed according to her instructions. Remember to make the change slowly—a sudden, dramatic shift in diet can cause digestive problems in your dog.

Chapter 7

Health and Housetraining

Before you start working on your dog's behavior, you need to make sure he's not housetrained due to a physical problem. Did you know there could be physical reasons why your dog is having accidents in the house? If that's the case, you can train your dog all you want, but it won't help because he will not be physically able to control himself.

Super Simple Tip

There are many physical ailments that can make housetraining difficult or impossible. If you're having housetraining troubles, have your vet determine whether a health problem is the cause.

Here's a quiz for you. (Don't worry, it's not hard!) Which of these statements best describes your dog?

1. My dog has always had accidents in the house. I can't really say he's ever gone for more than a short period of time without eliminating indoors.

2. My dog used to be housetrained; at least, I thought he was. He went months (or even years!) with no accidents, but now he's peeing in the house again.

If you picked #1, there's a good chance your issue may be behavioral. If your dog has always had accidents in the house, he's probably just never learned to eliminate outside. One thing to check: Does your dog pee frequently, seemingly every time you turn around?

Physical problems can affect your dog's ability to be housetrained.

Regular checkups will keep your dog in top condition.

If your dog is peeing frequently or seems thirsty all the time, you may want to check with your veterinarian to make sure there isn't something physical going on.

If you picked #2, then you definitely need to make sure there isn't a physical problem with your dog. Any time there is a sudden change in your dog's behavior, it's always a good idea to get your dog checked out by your veterinarian to rule out a health problem.

Sometimes pet owners get frustrated and angry at their dogs for suddenly peeing indoors, when it turns out their dogs really have urinary tract infections! Getting angry isn't fair to your dog and can damage your relationship if you yell at him for something he can't help. If you chose #2, call your veterinarian for an appointment today.

DISEASES THAT CAUSE INCONTINENCE

There are physical issues that can lead to incontinence in dogs. These issues may cause your dog to pee in your house and make it practically impossible to housetrain him. This is because your dog's body is working

Some medications cause incontinence. Keep a watchful eye on your dog whenever he is taking medication.

against you! You could be religiously following every tip in this book and it just won't help because your dog is ill. The top three incontinence culprits due to disease are:

- bladder stones
- tumors
- urinary tract infections (UTIs) (most common)

I don't want to scare you into thinking your dog may be sick, but you need to understand these issues so you can get early treatment if your dog needs it. How do you know if your dog has any of these problems? Here are the symptoms to look for:

- **Blood in urine.** You may notice the urine stream is pink or red.
- **Frequent urination.** Your dog is peeing much more often than usual.
- **Inappropriate elimination.** This basically means your dog would normally go outside to pee but is now peeing in the house. This is usually an early sign of a problem, which many dog owners mistake for stubbornness or spitefulness. I can't emphasize enough—if this behavior is unusual for your dog, then check to see if it's a physical problem first.
- **Small amounts.** Only a little urine comes out each time. You may wonder why you have to let your dog out so often, but it's because there's not much coming out of his bladder!
- **Straining.** When your dog assumes the position to pee, you may notice he seems to be having difficulty. He may whine or whimper. This is because it hurts when he urinates.
- **Urgency.** Your dog may be frantic to pee.

If you recognize any of these symptoms, please call your veterinarian. He or she may ask you to bring in a urine sample for testing. UTIs can

Getting a Urine Sample

Your veterinarian has asked you to bring in a urine sample. How in the heck do you get your dog to pee in a cup? Here are some tips for getting a good sample that will help your veterinarian help your dog.

First, you may want to pick up a box of disposable medical gloves. They are inexpensive, contain a generous amount in each box, are available at most discount department stores, and they come in very handy for dealing with this and other messy dog issues!

Make sure the sample goes into a clean container. Otherwise, the urine sample will have other things in it that may affect the results of testing.

For male dogs: The boys are a bit easier, because most of them lift their legs and give you easier access! Get a small plastic container with a snap-on lid that won't leak. Put on your gloves and take your dog out on leash to potty.

Give your dog the cue to potty, and when he goes, just hold the container in the urine stream. Collecting urine mid-stream is ideal, but don't worry about it if you don't manage to do that. You also don't need to get all of the urine or fill the container completely. Snap on the lid, clean the outside of the container, and you're set.

For female dogs: Girls are a bit harder because they generally squat to pee. And, especially if you have a toy breed dog, there's not a lot of room to reach in there for a sample! Get the lid of a long, flat plastic container. Make sure the lid has a lip to it that lets it snap onto the bottom part. Put on your gloves, take your girl out on leash, and give her the cue to potty.

When she starts to squat, quickly and quietly slide the lid of the container underneath her. She may startle and stop, but keep trying. Don't forget to praise her when she goes! You don't need to get all of the urine or fill the lid completely. The urine will go into the lid and collect in the groove of the lip, and you can then carefully transfer it to the container (or a smaller one if you wish).

You can keep a urine sample for up to 30 minutes at room temperature before it needs to be tested. If you can't work within that timeframe, then you should refrigerate the sample. You can also wait until you get to your veterinarian's office and take the sample in the parking lot. That way, the office can be sure the sample is fresh for testing.

If you are just not able to get a sample, your veterinarian can use a needle to extract it from your dog's bladder. This can be scary for your dog—although the sight of you chasing him with that container may be quite startling to your dog as well! It's a good idea to practice getting a urine sample in case the need arises.

be pretty common in dogs, and some dogs are even prone to contracting them again and again. The most common treatment for this is a round of antibiotics.

Bladder stones and tumors are less common, but they can cause incontinence problems, too. Your veterinarian will help you decide the best course of treatment for these issues.

There are other, less common diseases that can cause incontinence, including the following:

• diabetes
• Cushing's disease (a disease of the adrenal gland)
• kidney disease

How do you know if your dog has one of these diseases? One symptom is thirst, so you'll notice your dog drinking more. Then, because they're taking in more liquid, they have to get rid of more liquid! As a result, an afflicted dog will drink a lot and pee a lot. These symptoms will appear over time.

Dietary problems such as a food allergy, a sudden change in diet, or a food that's too rich for your pet can all cause him to have accidents.

Another problem some dogs experience is just plain incontinence. With this issue, your dog will wake up with a wet spot underneath him, indicating he's peed in his sleep. Some dogs don't even have to fall asleep; they'll pee after they become very relaxed. This issue is often treated with hormones.

DRUGS THAT CAUSE INCONTINENCE

Sometimes, drugs that your dog takes for illnesses can cause incontinence, too. You may be treating your dog for a problem completely unrelated to incontinence, but the treatment gives you a new problem! For example, let's say Fido is covered in welts because he has a flea allergy. His skin is so bad and painful that your veterinarian gives him a shot of a cortisone drug. His skin starts to clear, but you notice he's now peeing buckets all over your house! Having to go is a side effect of the drug.

Cortisone-type drugs (Prednisone, Dexamethasone, Depo-Medrol, etc.) often cause dogs to drink more and pee more than usual. If your dog is on this medication, please be patient and make sure you give more potty breaks than usual. Your dog can't help having to urinate more frequently!

Housetraining and the Older Dog

If you notice your senior dog suddenly having housetraining lapses where he was once completely reliable, you should first talk to your vet to make sure an illness isn't responsible. However, there's a chance that your dog is perfectly healthy and just needs to eliminate more frequently than he did in his younger years. Increase the number of times you take him out each day to accommodate his new needs, and remember not to get angry or punish him for accidents should they occur.

OH, POOP

Many physical issues cause dogs to pee in the house, but there are other problems that can cause your dog to poop as well. Again, if your dog was never really housetrained, you may find stools in your house. These should be firm stools. But if you're finding very loose stools or diarrhea, it's time to suspect a physical problem. Here are some common causes:

Some pills can cause incontinence in dogs.

1. **Diet.** Some diets may contribute to loose stools. Your dog may be allergic to an ingredient in the food he's eating. Maybe he's been eating people food and it's too rich for him. If you changed brands or the type of food he eats too quickly, then he may have an upset stomach, too. Whenever you change your dog's food, it's best to do it gradually, over at least a week. Some dogs just love eating odd things, like pinecones, bark, dirt, and even

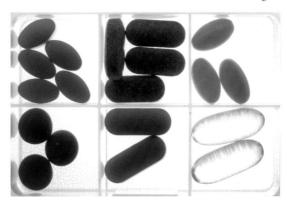

poop! This can cause his stomach bacteria to get all out of whack and give him an upset stomach as well.

Other than the loose stools, you'll also notice your dog has a real urgency to eliminate. If you're noticing these symptoms, please consult your veterinarian to rule out any serious problems.

2. **Parasites.** Parasites can also cause loose stools. There are a variety of worms that may infect your dog. Dogs mainly get worms from other dogs (except heartworms, which come from mosquitoes). Puppies contract them from their mothers, and dogs contract them from walking or getting into poop left behind from infected dogs. Worms can cause serious health problems for your dog.

Other parasites that can infect your dog are protozoans, or lower forms of life that get into your dog's system and cause all sorts of problems. If your dog enjoys lapping mud puddles, he could pick up some protozoans along with a drink!

There are treatments for parasites. Your veterinarian will first have to determine which parasite your dog has, and then he or she will

Diligence on your part can help solve your dog's house-training issues.

prescribe medication to kill the nasty things!

3. **Other medical problems.** Some dogs develop problems with their primary gastrointestinal tract, which can cause diarrhea.

OTHER PHYSICAL ISSUES THAT CAN CAUSE INCONTINENCE

The following are some other physical issues that can cause dogs to eliminate indoors.

Anal Gland Surgery

Some dogs develop chronic infections or cancer of the anal

Emotional issues such as stress can lead to housetraining problems in your dog.

glands, so some veterinarians may recommend removing them surgically. Not all, but some dogs that go through this surgery may lose control of their sphincter muscles. This means involuntary elimination may occur. If your dog has this problem, make sure he gets frequent potty breaks. Be extra patient with him because he can't help making a mess on occasion!

Spay Incontinence

Some female dogs that have been spayed may develop incontinence problems. After falling asleep, they may wake up to a wet spot underneath them. They may also have to pee when they get very relaxed. Spay incontinence is often treated with hormones.

Age

As dogs get older, they may have to eliminate more frequently. Sometimes this is just an age-related fact of life. Other times, though, age can subject a dog to other diseases, such as diabetes or urinary tract infections. If you notice your older dog having accidents in the house, don't automatically chalk it up to the golden years. Talk to your veterinarian and make sure it's not a problem that can be treated.

If a change in your environment is causing your dog stress, be patient with him.

If your veterinarian says your senior citizen is fine physically, then increase your dog's number of potty breaks each day. It seems we all have to go more frequently as we age.

MENTAL HEALTH AND HOUSETRAINING

If your dog was housetrained and suddenly began having accidents in the house, I've explained you should first check with your veterinarian. But what if your veterinarian has ruled out any physical problems? Should you assume it's a training problem? Not yet.

Before you get to training, take a good look at your environment. Is there anything stressful going on in your household? When dogs are stressed, one of the ways they show it is by having accidents indoors. Dogs are very much creatures of routine, so if their routines are changed, they may become stressed. For example, are there any changes in the number of people in your home, like a new baby? Maybe you're dating someone new, or you just broke up with a long-term significant other. It could be something as simple as having your in-laws staying over the holidays! Dogs also feel loss when you lose another pet. If your dog was best friends with another canine buddy and that dog is now gone, you may notice some behavioral changes in him. Your dog will even feel tensions that may exist in the home.

If you realize there is a change in your environment that could be causing your dog stress, then be patient with him. If he's having accidents in your house, he's not being spiteful or trying to get back at you for anything. He's just upset! And while you may snap at someone or burst into tears when you're unhappy, dogs express themselves differently. When they're upset, they may chew on inappropriate items or eliminate indoors.

To help your dog, stick to a routine as much as possible. Give him more frequent potty breaks until things settle down. Increase his exercise, which will let him run off some stress and also improve his physical health. Most of all, let him know you love him! If you let him know you're okay, then he soon will be, too.

Age can be a contributing factor to a dog having accidents in the house.

When You Know It's a Behavioral Issue

If you've read this entire section and nothing sounds like what your dog is experiencing, and your veterinarian has cleared your dog of any health problems that could be interfering with your housetraining efforts, then it's time to tackle your dog's potty problems from a behavior standpoint!

Part Four

How to Housetrain

Chapter 8

Time to Train

At first, housetraining may seem quite tedious. You'll have to supervise, supervise, and then supervise some more. You'll have to work with your dog, rather than asking him to figure things out on his own. But putting forth this effort now will really pay off in the long run! Please don't be discouraged, because you won't have to be so diligent forever. Just remember the first time you learned to do something, like ride a bike. At first, you had training wheels. Then, when the training wheels came off, an adult probably held the bike until you learned to balance yourself. That adult had to stay beside you every step of the way, holding onto that bike! In the end, the effort worked, because once you learned to ride the bike, you didn't need someone following you all the time. Keep that in mind as you housetrain your dog.

Super Simple Tip

The best way to prevent your dog from eliminating indoors is to never give him a chance to. Keep him under close supervision—or in his crate when you can't watch him.

Housetraining will be more successful if there are no distractions.

At first, you're going to be working closely with your dog to show him exactly what you want. You have to make things very clear for him so he won't misinterpret anything. As you both fall into your routines, be consistent and he'll figure out exactly what you want. Plus, you won't have to stay on top of him all the time. It's important, then, to begin with a lot of supervision and effort; as your dog improves, you can gradually taper off. Sounds simple, doesn't it? It really is!

SUPERVISING YOUR DOG

In order to set your dog up for success, you're going to have to manage his environment so that he doesn't even have a chance to practice behavior you don't like—in this case, eliminating inside the house. If your dog never has a chance to eliminate inside your house and only has opportunities to eliminate outside, then you're creating a consistent, positive educational environment. He'll get into the habit of going outside to eliminate because he'll know that's all he ever can do, and he'll realize he's rewarded for it every time. It's up to you to make sure he never has a chance to have an accident.

Prevention means watching your dog like a hawk. I'm not kidding. It doesn't take long for your dog—especially if you have a toy breed—to pee on your floor. For every accident he has inside, your dog is practicing behavior you don't want, and you're both taking a step backwards in training. Even a few seconds without supervision can set back your training. Sound daunting? Once you get into the habit of watching your dog and managing his environment, it'll become a new habit for you, too! You'll be learning this new routine together.

INTRODUCING THE CRATE

A crate is a wonderful tool for housetraining your dog because it allows him to be safe and secure during times when you can't supervise him. But what if your dog has never spent any time in a crate? Not a problem. You'll just have to gradually introduce it as a positive, fun place for him.

Please, never use the crate for punishment. If you yell at your dog and toss him in the crate when you're angry, he'll learn to associate the crate with bad things only. You want him to learn that his crate is a safe den.

Commit to housetraining your dog. No matter the weather, when he has to go, make sure he does it outside!

Step 1:

A. Put the crate where your dog will be near your family. If you put him away in a laundry room where you hardly ever go, your dog will feel alone. You want to keep him as part of the family, not make him feel like an outsider! This means the best place to put a crate is where your family hangs out.

B. Decide what cue you want to use when your dog goes into his crate. You'll use this cue every single time. Some suggestions include "go to kennel" or "kennel up" or "go to bed." If your sense of humor dictates, you could even try "go to jail." It doesn't matter what cue you use, just make sure you (and your family) use the same cue for this specific action every time. It does help to keep the phrase short. Saying, "Hurry up and go into your kennel before you pee on the floor yet another time!" is not something that your dog can associate with an action very easily!

C. When you cannot watch your dog, he should be in his crate. Headed to work for the day? Crate your dog. Preparing dinner and busy in the kitchen? Crate your dog. It does seem like a lot of time at first, but as your dog gains better control, then he'll be able to spend more and

A crate allows you to keep your dog safe and secure when you can't keep an eye on him.

more time out of his crate.

D. Make sure your dog's crate is safe. If you have a wire crate, do not leave your dog's collar on—it could get caught on the wire. Only leave safe toys in there with him. Also, make sure the crate is not near something he can pull into it. Some dogs have been known to drag neighboring tablecloths, electrical wires, and other assorted dangerous items into their crates if they can reach them!

If you have a young dog that is an enthusiastic chewer or even an older dog that is still destructive, do not leave any blankets or bedding in his crate unless you are sure he won't shred and eat them.

Step 2:

A. Start gradually. Don't just toss your dog in the crate and shut the door, or he may end up fearing the crate. Build up slowly.

B. Leave the crate open and toss some treats in there when you pass by throughout the day. Let your dog go in after the treats. When he does, praise him! Don't shut the door behind him yet.

C. For all of his meals, get his meal ready, put the bowl in the crate, and shut the door—with the dog outside of the crate! Wait about five minutes for him to build up some anticipation; then let him in the crate with the cue "go to kennel." Let him eat his meal without shutting the door behind him.

Step 3:

If your dog is now eagerly going into his crate, you are ready for Step 3. If he still resists, spend some more time on Step 2. Pushing your dog too fast will undo all of your hard work!

A. Get a treat in your hand. Show it to your dog and give him the "go to kennel" cue (or whatever cue you have chosen). Then, use the treat in your hand to lure him into the crate. If he follows it in, give him the treat when he gets into the crate and praise him! Do this several times a day.

   If he does not follow the treat lure into the crate, go back to Step 2 for a little while and then try again. This time, though, use better treats!

B. Now that your dog is happily going into his crate, start shutting the door for a few minutes and then let him out, but only if he's being quiet and not barking or pawing at the door. If he barks and whines and you let him out, you are teaching your dog that whining gets him free! Oops! Always make sure he's behaving when you let him out so he'll learn that good manners bring rewards.

C. Gradually increase the time your dog stays in his crate. Begin with a few minutes, then a half hour, then an hour. Make sure to give him plenty of breaks in between your crate training sessions.

Make your dog's crate comfortable so that he'll feel at home.

D. Gradually work up to longer times in the crate. Vary your routine; sometimes leave him in the crate when you are home and just puttering around the house instead of just when you leave. Otherwise, your puppy may start associating the crate with you leaving the house, which could make it a negative experience.

The Importance of Exercise

When you are first housetraining your dog, he may be in his crate for long periods of time, especially if you're starting with a puppy. It's extremely important your dog get the right amount of exercise, quality time, and affection outside his crate. This is what separates the crate as a useful tool from turning into something cruel!

Many people do not understand just how much exercise their dogs need to stay healthy. Think of the average Labrador or Golden Retriever. These dogs were originally bred to hunt, dive into ponds and lakes, run through brush, and retrieve dead game. The average Border Collie and Australian Shepherd were originally bred to chase and herd hundreds of sheep over rough terrain every single day. If you don't hunt, or if you don't happen to have a herd of sheep in your backyard, it doesn't mean your dog's original blueprint changes. Many of the dogs today still have the same needs their forefathers did, and a brisk walk twice around the block won't cut it!

If your dog is very bouncy, always on the go, and constantly getting into trouble, and if you can't easily feel your dog's ribs when you run your hands lightly down his sides, then your dog is probably not getting the proper amount of exercise for his age and breed/breed combination.

A lack of exercise is just as bad for dogs as it is for us humans. It also causes behavior problems. Take a Labrador, for instance. If you don't give this smart dog a job, he'll get bored. And a bored dog is one that will find ways to amuse himself, even if that means shredding your couch! Leaving a dog outside all day does not give him exercise. Usually, your dog will run around for a couple of minutes, then lie down and wait for you to get home!

Think about what type of dog you chose to bring home and the original job he was bred to do. If you have a mixed breed, think about the different breeds that make up your dog, as best as you know. Then, talk to your veterinarian and a professional dog trainer about the proper amount of exercise for your dog's type, age, and physical fitness level. For example, some sports, like agility, require a dog to be physically developed before he can safely perform certain exercises. If your dog is not used to proper exercise, you'll need to build him up gradually so you don't put undue stress on his muscles, joints, and bones. The exercise you choose may end up being a 30-minute game of fetch twice a day, or dates three times a week for puppy playtime with other friendly dogs. Making sure your dog gets enough exercise will keep him healthy and help your overall training program!

Step 4:

By now your dog should be running into his crate when you give him the cue and staying in there for appropriate amounts of time. If not, then go back to Step 3 and work some more until you're ready to move onto this step.

Slow and Steady

If your dog is new to the crate, introduce him to it slowly, rewarding him for every small step in the right direction. If you rush your dog's crate training, he'll be more likely to fear the crate.

A. Now it's time to stop using a cookie to lure your dog into his crate. Instead, give him the "go to kennel" cue and point to his crate as if you have a cookie in your hand. This is not to fool your dog. Dogs have an incredible sense of smell—they know you don't have a treat in your hand. Instead, what you are doing is using the same hand signal you've actually been teaching your dog all along. Dogs learn body language much faster than verbal language. If you use your hands in the same way, your dog will better understand

Once your dog learns that the crate is his home, he should have an easier time being housetrained.

what you want of him.

B. As soon as he goes into the crate, praise him! Shut the door, quickly get a treat, and give it to him through the crate door. This will teach your dog that you may not always have treats with you, but he should still do what you ask because he'll be rewarded!

Crates in Toyland

When you're initially housetraining your dog, he may be confined a lot of the time until he learns the ropes. But this doesn't mean he should live in a bare bones barrack— turn his crate into toyland!

Dogs need to keep mentally and physically active. There are lots of toys on the market that can help your dog become more active and make his confinement much more pleasant.

However, the quantity of toys isn't as important as the quality. Dogs can easily get bored by the same toys, even if they have dozens to choose from. Basically, you don't have to buy out the pet store. Instead, have at least two sets of toys on hand and rotate them every week or so. Your dog will be less likely to get used to the toys this way and may even act like they're new toys every time.

If your dog will be unsupervised in his crate, then it's important that all toys you leave with him are safe. Ask your veterinarian or a professional dog trainer for ideas. Some toys that are safe for some dogs are not safe for other dogs. It all depends on how destructive your particular dog is. For example, one dog could have the same stuffed animal his entire life, while another dog might rip it to pieces in search of the squeaker in 30 seconds!

Also, make sure the toys you choose are the right size for your dog. Especially watch growing puppies—they get big pretty fast, and a toy that was perfect at three months may be dangerously small when they're six months old.

In general, hard rubber hollow toys that you can stuff with peanut butter and dry kibble are usually popular choices. Nylon bones, such as those made by Nylabone, can help ease your dog's need to chew. Sterilized beef bones stuffed with goodies are usually tough enough for the most enthusiastic chewer. Just know your dog and take away any toy that looks damaged or has been worn down so much that it could be swallowed. You want your dog to be entertained in his crate, but safely!

Dogs learn body language much faster than verbal language.

COMMON CRATE TRAINING CHALLENGES

Here are some common challenges in crate training:

"My dog doesn't seem to like his crate at all! He cries and whines when I put him in there."

There could be several reasons why your dog does not enjoy his den.

- You may have gone too fast in your training. Your dog should enjoy each step before you proceed to the next one. Just back up to a step where he was successful and try again, this time more slowly.
- Where is his crate? Is it near the family? Dogs that are left alone feel left out! Some people choose to have one crate for the main family room and another for the bedroom for overnight. Whether or not you choose to keep your dog in the bedroom is up to you, although many dogs enjoy feeling close to where you sleep. Sometimes just moving the crate to a place of family activity can help ease your dog's stress, so he won't feel a need to whine!
- Be sure you leave your dog's favorite toys in there with him. One favorite is a rubber toy filled with peanut butter and dry kibble. It's like

a doggie pacifier!

- Make sure you're not using the crate for punishment. This will teach your dog the crate is a bad place, not a good one.
- It's also important not to leave your dog in his crate longer than is reasonable. For example, if you have a nine-week-old puppy, it's unrealistic to think he can hold his bladder for eight hours in his crate! He may try to hold it, but his body just won't let him. This can lead to health problems, like urinary tract infections. It will also teach your dog to potty in his crate because he physically has no choice.

"When I reach for the door to let my dog out, he starts barking and paws at the door. It's obnoxious!"

Freeze. Do nothing, and especially don't reach for the door! If you let your dog out of his crate when he's acting obnoxiously, he'll learn that's what it takes to get what he wants. And that's a lesson you'll soon regret! If you freeze, your dog will have to stop acting like a maniac sometime. The second that he does, immediately reach for the door again. He will probably start barking again. Just freeze again. He'll soon learn that if he's barking and pawing at the crate door, your hand will never move. He's smart—you just have to be smarter!

"My dog likes his crate fine, but he pees on his blanket every day!"

First, make sure your dog is not in his crate any longer than is reasonable. If you're doing well with that, then remove the blanket. Some dogs will pee on a blanket, ball it up in a corner, and stay high and dry the rest of the day. This is not teaching them to avoid soiling their dens at all. Rather than doing dog laundry every afternoon, just take away blanket privileges until your dog better understands the crate training concept.

"I crate my dog all day and he does fine. But at night, I want him to sleep with me. Sometimes I wake up and there's pee on the floor. Is there anything I can do?"

Sure! You can crate your dog until he's completely housetrained. If your dog is having accidents in the house, then he's not ready for that much freedom yet. That doesn't mean he won't earn it eventually, but you are just setting back your training by allowing him to take a potty break when you're fast asleep and can't catch him in the act. You're actually teaching him that it's okay to pee in your bedroom. Oops!

Do your dog a favor. First, train him. Then you can have a bed buddy if you wish!

"I tried crate training in the past, but I think I made some mistakes and now my dog doesn't like his crate. I want to try again...how do I start?"

It may help to buy a different kind of crate. Your dog already associates the old crate with unpleasant things, so it might be useful to start with a crate that looks completely different. It may

Even if your dog likes his crate, don't leave him in there for too long a time.

also help to put the new crate in a different part of your home—anything to make housetraining seem new and not remind him of old experiences.

Start crate training from scratch. Make it a very positive experience and follow the steps I've outlined. Just because your dog didn't like a crate before doesn't mean he can't learn to like one now. Be extra patient with him and make the experience fun!

Chapter 9

Super Supervision: When You Need to Get Closer

For many dogs, the crate is enough to teach them not to eliminate in their den. Next, you're going to transfer this knowledge to the rest of your home. But some dogs are just super speedy piddlers! You might turn away for just a second, and that's all the time they'll need to pee on your rug. Some toy breed dogs fall into this category because they're just so fast!

Once your dog has learned not to eliminate in his crate, you can give him more freedom in the house.

If you find your dog having accidents despite your best attempts at supervision, then it's time to get closer. A lot closer. Put your dog on leash and tie the leash to your belt loop. You'll be attached to your dog, so he won't have a chance to sneak off and have an accident. You'll be able to watch him more closely, too, because he'll be close by and you can watch for signs that he has to eliminate.

Don't worry; you won't have to walk around with a dog attached to you for the rest of your life! What will happen is that you'll be watching your dog more closely, so you'll be able to prevent him from eliminating in your home. In fact, you'll be catching him before he even has a chance to go! You'll be able to take him out more often, and you'll reward him every time he potties outside. As your dog learns that it's more rewarding to go outside every time, he'll form that habit (instead of the one where he waits for you to turn your back so he can pee on the rug).

GETTING ON SCHEDULE

While you're teaching your dog to love his crate, you need to set up a routine schedule because dogs are very much creatures of habit. If you take your dog for a walk every evening for a couple of months, then try to skip a night, what happens? Your dog acts like you've lost your mind! He may run to the door and back to you, he may even go get his leash or bark at you. That's because you're interrupting his routine. You can use this to your advantage by setting up a routine for your dog to help you with your housetraining.

First, set up a feeding schedule. By controlling when your dog takes in food and water, you can control when the food and water has to come out! Set up regular times and try to stick to them as closely as possible. For puppies six months and younger, figure on three meals a day. Feed adult dogs twice a day.

Now it's time to think about the number of potty breaks your dog will need. If you have a young puppy, you'll need to include more frequent potty breaks. In general, puppies need to eliminate as soon as they wake up in the morning, after they eat, and after they wake up from a nap. They also have to go right after rigorous playtime. Have you been playing fetch or tug with your puppy for a bit? He will probably need to potty. Does your puppy get the "zoomies"? That's when your pup seems to go completely insane, running around the house like a mad dog, with

Until your dog gets used to his schedule, be prepared for accidents to happen.

Set up a schedule with plenty of outside time so that your pup learns better.

eyes happily glazed. This is not something to be alarmed about, it's just something that puppies do (sometimes the behavior carries into adulthood, too), and they usually need to potty right afterwards. Puppies also often have to go right after a bath.

An important thing to remember is that puppies don't have much bladder control yet, so when they have to go, they have to go! They won't wait for a ballgame inning to be over or a commercial to come on television. They sometimes can't even wait for you to tie your shoes! Get ready to sprint if you have a youngster because he won't be able to hold it.

Activities aside, the younger the puppy, the more frequently he will need a potty break. A puppy that is only eight weeks old will need to go out every one to two hours; a puppy that is four months old will have to go out about every four hours; and a six-month-old puppy will be able to hold it in his crate for about six to seven hours maximum.

Adult dogs do not have to eliminate as often, although when you're starting your training program you'll have more potty breaks than usual to help him learn his new routine.

ESTABLISHING A SCHEDULE

When making your schedule, you need to look at your lifestyle and your puppy or adult dog's needs. Is there someone home all day? If the answer is yes, then housetraining will be a breeze because someone will be there to let your dog outside frequently. The majority of folks work outside the home, however. This can be a greater challenge. If you have a puppy six months or younger and you work an eight- to nine-hour day, your puppy cannot physically hold it all day in his crate. You have a couple of choices:

Super Simple Tip

Set up a feeding schedule to help your puppy eliminate at regular intervals.

1. Come home midday to give your puppy a potty break.
   Benefits: You'll keep your dog on schedule, and your housetraining will succeed much faster. And puppy therapy is a great way to break up a busy workday! You'll be much happier when you get back to the office.
   What to Watch: Your boss may not love this plan, but perhaps you can work out a deal to come in early or stay late to take an extended lunch. If you can last until your puppy turns six months old with a consistent housetraining schedule, then you should be able to skip the midday potty breaks. Then again, you may find you don't want to skip them after you've gotten used to the break with your best friend!

2. Ask a neighbor, friend, or family member to come in during the day and let your dog out for a potty break.
   Benefits: As long as everyone sticks to the training plan, your dog will keep on schedule, so it'll make housetraining easier. Plus, he'll get social time with other people.
   What to Watch: Just make sure everyone follows the same training plan.

3. Hire a pet sitter to come in during the day and let your dog out for a potty break.
   Benefits: You'll pay someone to keep your dog on schedule, so it'll make housetraining easier. Plus, he'll get social time with other people.
   What to Watch: Just make sure you hire a quality pet sitter. Ask

your veterinarian, dog trainer, and friends for references.

4. Take your dog to "doggie daycare."
   Benefits: Great fun, exercise, and socialization for your dog.
   What to Watch: Not all doggie daycares are quality places, so make sure the owners know dog behavior and are willing to help you train your dog with reward-based methods.

5. Leave your dog outside in a fenced yard when you're at work.
   Benefits: Your dog will not eliminate in the house.
   What to Watch: Leaving a dog outside all day can lead to behavioral issues, such as barking at neighbors and destroying

When There's No Way for a Midday Puppy Potty Break

Giving a puppy less than six months of age a midday potty break is just part of the package of puppy ownership. But what if you can't find someone to give your puppy a midday break or if you can't afford a pet sitter or doggie daycare? If you can, try a combination of the choices I've outlined. Maybe you can come home twice a week during your lunch break, and a friend can check in on Fido three times a week. Or maybe you can trade pet sitting duties for babysitting duties with a neighbor!

If you've exhausted all your options and you just can't make a midday potty break happen, then realize your housetraining efforts will be more challenging because you'll be giving your puppy mixed signals. A young puppy will have to eliminate indoors, so it'll be harder to teach him to only eliminate outdoors.

If you crate your dog, he will probably learn to eliminate in the crate because he can't hold it that long. This means he could learn that it's okay to hang out in his waste all day. This is not a healthy lesson! It's probably better to enclose a larger, safe area in your home as a last resort. You can purchase an exercise pen for this purpose or close off a safe room with a baby gate.

Get a litter box and put sod in it, with grass. Put it in a corner of his area, away from his water bowl and bed. This at least resembles an outside environment, rather than newspapers or potty pads. Remember, you won't be there to teach him what to do, and Fido can't read your mind! Hopefully, he'll learn to go on the sod in the litter box. If you get some of his urine or waste, you can put it on the sod as an incentive for him to eliminate there. As he gets older and doesn't need to eliminate as frequently, you'll be able to adjust his schedule to better fit your busy one.

Puppies don't have much control over their bladders, so take them outside soon after their meals.

your plants. Dogs can get loose, which isn't safe. And it's horrible to think about, but some communities have a real problem with dog thefts! Neighborhood bullies or unfriendly children can also torment dogs behind a fence, which can lead to fear and aggression issues. If this is your best option, please weigh it carefully, and make sure your dog has proper shelter and is secure in your yard, away from danger.

Sample Schedules

With everyone's busy schedules, most people can't wait to stop those midday breaks! However, if you are able to continue them after your dog is old enough and housetrained, then by all means consider doing so. It'll be a nice break for your dog!

Here are a couple of sample schedules.

5-Month-Old Puppy, Not Housetrained. Owner Works Outside of Home.

7:30 a.m. Potty break.

7:40 a.m. Feed puppy breakfast.

7:50 a.m. Potty break. Put puppy in crate.

8:30 a.m. Owner leaves for work.

12:30 p.m. Neighbor gives puppy potty break.

12:40 p.m. Neighbor gives puppy midday meal.

12:45 p.m. Neighbor gives puppy potty break. Puts puppy in crate.

5:30 p.m. Owner arrives home. Potty break.

6:30 p.m. Potty break.

7:30 p.m. Feed puppy dinner.

7:40 p.m. Potty break.

9:00 p.m. Potty break. Take up water so puppy can better hold bladder all night.

10:00 p.m. Final potty break. Puppy goes in crate for the night.

When making up a housetraining schedule, take your dog's type, age, and activities into consideration.

With this schedule, you'll see there are nine potty breaks. That's nine chances each day to practice eliminating outside! Of course, if you have a family member at home, you won't need to enlist your neighbor's help for the midday break. Remember to factor in your dog's type, age, and activities. Let's say your puppy plays a rousing game of fetch at 5:45 p.m. You should take him outside right afterwards because he may have to go again! If you have a toy breed, waiting from 7:40 p.m. until 9:00 p.m. may be too long—you may want to take your toy puppy out at 8:15 p.m. instead. This is just an outline of what a potty schedule may look like. Let's look at another one.

Two-Year-Old Dog, Not Housetrained. Owner Works Outside of Home.

7:30 a.m. Potty break.

7:40 a.m. Feed dog breakfast.

7:50 a.m. Put dog in crate.

8:30 a.m. Owner leaves for work.

5:30 p.m. Owner arrives home. Potty break.

7:00 p.m. Potty break.

Make sure all members of the family follow the training schedule.

7:30 p.m. Feed dog dinner.
7:40 p.m. Potty break.
10:00 p.m. Final potty break. Dog goes in crate for the night.

With this schedule, there are five potty breaks. This is because an adult dog can physically hold his bladder and bowels better than a young puppy. Again, take into consideration your dog's type, age, and activities.

If he is a toy breed, you may need some more frequent breaks. As your dog learns to be housetrained, he may need fewer potty breaks. This doesn't mean your goal is to only take him out once a day! It just means the closer you stick to your schedule, the more he'll learn it. In fact, you both may get so good at this that you'll know if something is wrong with your dog's urinary tract or digestive system much earlier than before, because it'll stand out as different from your daily routine.

Chapter 10

Outdoor Training

Training your dog to go outside is the easiest part of your journey. It's really not complicated at all. It's the scheduling, routine, feeding, consistency, and other issues that seem to be the most common barriers to success. But you've already got a handle on that, right? So let's move on to the next step!

It's important to reward your dog for positive behaviors during training sessions.

When training your dog to do anything, it's important to reward him immediately for behavior you like. This means you're going to have to go outside with your dog, so you can reward him for eliminating outside the second he does so. If you wait until he comes inside afterwards and praise him then, you're really praising him for coming in the door!

Here is how to train your dog to go outside to potty:

Step 1:

A. Attach a leash to your dog. If you're not attached to your dog, you can't control the environment, so he could end up running all over your backyard!

B. Hide a couple of small treats in your hand. Make sure they're something he really likes.

Step 2:

A. Take your dog outside. If you want, you can put a cue on this as well, such as "wanna go outside?" If you use the same cue every time with the same action, your dog will learn to associate the two.

B. Watch your dog for signs he has to eliminate: sniffing the ground, assuming the position to go, etc. As soon as he starts, give him your cue to potty: "Go potty!" "Do your business!" Say whatever you want, just make sure you use the same cue every time.

C. When he's done, praise him! A simple "good dog" won't cut it—make him know you're thrilled with his performance! Give him a cookie and tell him he's wonderful.

Helpful Hints:

- If you have a puppy, be advised that puppies often have to go twice. This means Fido may pee or poop in one spot and then walk around a bit and pee and poop in another spot.

- Give your dog an allotted amount of time to find the right spot. If you want him to learn to do his business within five minutes, then only give him five minutes. Be consistent. Don't give him 30 minutes on Saturday and then get frustrated when he takes 30 minutes Monday morning.

How you deal with your dog's accidents will affect your success in training.

Step 3:

A. If you want Fido to now play in his fenced yard, take off his leash and give him another cue, such as "go play!" By making sure he potties first, he learns to get it out of the way before playtime. This comes in handy, especially when traveling or on bad weather days when he can't play outside! He'll learn to do his business quickly right off the bat.

B. If he does not go within your

allotted time, bring him back inside and put him in his crate for 15 minutes. Then try again from Step 1. If he's confined, he will be less likely to have an accident in the house. If you're able to watch him very carefully, then you can do that, instead.

ACCIDENTS HAPPEN

Despite your best efforts, it's likely your dog will have a few accidents along the way. How you deal with them will affect your success in training.

Old-fashioned training used to recommend rubbing your dog's nose in his mess or spanking your dog. However, these methods do not teach your dog to eliminate outside. Instead, they can teach him to be afraid of you! He'll probably think you've completely lost your marbles.

If you find an accident in the house and you did not catch your dog eliminating, then there's nothing you can do but clean it up. Be sure to use a proper cleanser so he won't want to go back to the same spot again and again. Think about your supervision technique and see how you can improve it. Does your dog have too much freedom in the house? Is he not getting enough potty breaks for his age and type? See where the mistake is

Your dog may be eliminating in the house because he has too much freedom there.

A reward and praise will let your dog know that you are pleased with his performance.

in the training and then fix it.

If you do catch your dog having an accident, use your voice to interrupt the behavior with a sharp, "No!" That's all you need. Immediately grab his leash, hook it to his collar, and whisk him outside.

Once he's outside, give him his cue to potty. If he finishes outside, praise and treat! It's tempting to give him a stern lecture about the perils of peeing inside, but this will go against your training. This is because he's now doing what you want—going outside—so you need to make it very clear that you love it when this happens! Then, bring him back inside and put him in his crate while you clean up the mess. Again, lecturing your dog now will do you no good; if you do, he'll think you're mad at him for coming back inside!

The goal is to make things crystal clear to your dog. You hate it when he goes inside. You love it when he goes outside! If he has an accident indoors, your voice will tell him in no uncertain terms that he has displeased you. When he goes outside, your voice, treats, and show of affection will let him know you're thrilled! Dogs will repeat what works. If

A distracted puppy may forget why you brought him outside in the first place.

they get rewarded for going outside, they'll do it more often.

If your dog has accidents, please don't be too discouraged. This is normal. Dogs can go for three weeks with no accidents like housetrained angels, and then you may suddenly find pee under the dining room table. They're learning. Learning takes time and patience. If you stick with the program, you can succeed!

COMMON OUTDOOR TRAINING CHALLENGES

Here are some common challenges in outdoor training:

"My dog seems to be doing well going outside...except when it rains. He just goes out the door, looks miserable, and won't do a thing! What can I do?"

Some dogs could pee outside during a hurricane and not blink an eye, but some dogs hate rainy weather. Think about it—it's not very appealing to do your business outside with no protection from the elements, either! If you have a dog that thinks he'll melt in the rain, consider taking him out with an umbrella. You may feel a bit indulgent, but you won't have pee on your carpet! You can also think about putting up a small shelter in your backyard where your dog can dart under to do his business.

Another thing to consider is his reward. What tasty goodie will he get

It's a Material Thing

Did you know that some dogs could develop a preference for certain materials on which to eliminate? When those dogs end up in an environment that doesn't feature their favorite material, they may refuse to go!

Let's say you're traveling with your dog. You take a rest stop, and the pet-designated area is covered with pine straw. Your dog sniffs and sniffs but doesn't go. It's been ages since he last went and you know he has to potty, but he just looks confused. It's like he's looking for the perfect spot that never appears. Is he deliberately trying to make you late on your trip? Not at all. If he's used to a typical suburban yard with grass, then he may not be used to going on pine straw.

This is not unusual. Some dogs that are well trained to potty outside at home seem to be horrified at the thought of going on material that's different from their home turf. It's true; some dogs just seem to be prissier than others. But most of them that do this are just plain confused.

What if you want to travel with your dog? You can't possibly guarantee what kind of surface will be available wherever you go. Your dog may have to learn to eliminate on pine straw, gravel, concrete, or even sawdust! Fortunately, you can train your dog to go on different surfaces. First, train your dog to go on cue, as I've described. If you time the cue correctly by saying the words just as your dog performs the action, then your dog will associate those specific words with that action.

Next, take your dog to different areas and use your cue. Your dog will be familiar with your cue, but he may not want to go on different surfaces at first. Be sure to set your dog up for success! Pick a time when you know he'll have to go. If you know this will be difficult for him, take along some extra special treats to reward him.

Be patient when training this technique. There are people who prefer certain types of bathrooms, too!

if he does his business outside? If it's a bright sunny day, a regular dry biscuit may be a perfectly suitable paycheck. But if it's monsoon season and it's raining rivers out there, up the ante! Give your boy a piece of beef or liver for eliminating outside. It was harder for him to go under those conditions, so he should get some hardship pay!

"I have a three-and-a-half-month-old puppy, and he always walks right next to me. Do I have to use a leash when I take him out to potty?"

It's a good idea. Your puppy is young, and he is following you around like a little duckling. But he'll soon grow up! Right now, he doesn't really notice the squirrel dancing on your fence, the neighborhood children running down the street, or the traffic whizzing by. But soon he'll start becoming more aware of his surroundings, and he'll want to explore them. Many owners are shocked the day their pup dashes out into the street, because up until that point he never left their sides.

If you have a fenced yard, it's not so much a problem with danger as it is focus. If you're attached to your puppy and he gets distracted and wants to chase grasshoppers, you can gently lead him away from temptation and help him focus on the business at hand.

If you have several dogs that are left unsupervised in the house, it can be hard to tell which one is having accidents.

"I have a young puppy, and when I take him outside, he goes. But then he goes again as soon as I bring him inside! What am I doing wrong?"

Many young puppies have to go twice in a row. Give your puppy a chance to go the first time, and praise him! Then give him a few more minutes to walk around and stimulate his digestive system to go again. You may have to give him some more time to get everything out of his system.

Super Simple Tip

To get your dog on a definitive housetraining schedule, give him a set amount of time in which to eliminate.

"My dog stays with my parents during the day. They put newspaper down on the floor for him to potty on. I don't want to use newspaper at my house and would prefer he go outside. Is this going to confuse him?"

Probably. You're asking your dog to learn two different methods. If he stays at your parents' house every weekday but spends weeknights with you, you're asking him to learn them both on a daily basis! In one house, he's learning it's okay to pee and poop on newspaper. In the other, he's learning to pee and poop outside. This can be very confusing for a dog to understand, because the methods conflict with each other. He could be at your house and pee on the newspaper you're reading, and you can't get mad at him, because your folks taught him it was okay!

Try getting your parents on the same training path. Explain why you don't want your dog to eliminate on newspaper, and ask them to help you train him. Sometimes it can be harder to train people than dogs! But if the entire family gets on the same game plan, your dog will learn housetraining much faster.

"I have multiple dogs, and when I come home from work I find pee on the carpet. I don't know which one is having an accident. I suspect it's the younger one, but how can I be sure?"

If you have several dogs that are left unsupervised in your home, it can be difficult to tell which one is having accidents. It's a danger to suspect just one, because oftentimes people are surprised at the culprit! And what if they're taking turns?

If you really can't determine which dog is having accidents in the

Puppies often have to eliminate twice in a row.

home, then housetrain all the dogs from scratch. This way you'll train all your dogs, and the guilty party can't pass the blame!

THE LITTER BOX OPTION

In Chapter 5, I explained that litter box training was the least confusing alternative for your toy or small breed dog if you didn't want him to eliminate outside. Kittens instinctively know how to use a litter box, but your dog won't understand the concept that quickly!

If you want to use a litter box, you just have to modify the regular outdoor training steps to fit this option:

Step 1:

A. Carry your toy dog to the litter box, or attach a leash and gently lead him there. If you're not going to leash him, then make sure he can't escape the room the litter box is in until your potty session is over. Toy breed dogs seem to be really good at peeing while they run, so if you end up chasing him, you could end up with a piddle trail down the hallway!

B. Hide a couple of small treats in your hand. Make sure they're something he really likes.

Step 2:

A. Watch your dog for signs he has to eliminate: sniffing the litter, assuming the position to go, etc. As soon as he starts, give him your cue to potty: "Go potty!" "Do your business!" Say whatever you want, just make sure you use the same cue every time.

B. When he's done, praise him! A simple "good dog" won't cut it—make him know you're thrilled with his performance! Give him a cookie and tell him he's wonderful.

Helpful Hints:

- If you have a puppy, be advised that puppies often have to go twice. This means Fido may pee or poop in one spot, then walk around a bit and pee and poop in another.

- Give your dog an allotted amount of time. If you want him to learn to do his business within five minutes, then only give him five minutes. Be consistent. Don't give him 30 minutes one Saturday, and then get frustrated when he takes 30 minutes Monday morning.

Step 3:

A. If you want Fido to now play indoors, you can give him another cue, like "go play!" Then take off his leash or open the door.

B. If he does not go within your allotted time, put him in his crate for 15 minutes. Then try again from Step 1. If he's confined, he will be less likely to have an accident in the house. If you're able to watch him very carefully, then you can do that, instead. But really watch those little guys—they can pee in a flash!

Chapter 11

Recognizing and Training Signals to Go Out

Some dogs are very obvious when they have to go out. They may whine at you, paw at you, bark at you, then run to the door. They may bark at the door. They may paw or scratch at the door. They practically send up flares! Other dogs do have signals, but they're so subtle you may not catch them. They may quietly look at you, then at the door. If you miss the look, you miss the signal. However, not every dog comes with a built-in signal. Many dogs have no signal at all. But if you want, you can teach your dog to let you know when he has to eliminate outside. It's easy!

Dogs don't always let you know when they need to go outside, but you can train them to signal you.

Step 1:

A. First, pick a signal. Be careful what you wish for…if you get excited that your dog scratches at the door, will you stay excited when there's nothing but deep grooves left in your doorway? You may think it's great your dog barks at you to go outside, but will it be as appealing first thing in the morning? You may not mind your dog pawing at you as a signal, but what about pawing at your child or your elderly mother who watches your dog when you're out of town?

Be sure to choose a signal you can live with for a long time. One popular choice is a bell. You can pick up a bell at most any craft store, especially during the holidays. Get a medium or large-sized jingle bell, and attach it to a ribbon or piece of twine. The ribbon should be long enough so that your dog will be able to reach the bell with a paw when you hang it on the doorknob.

B. Choose a door you'll use to take your dog outside every time. Hang the bell from this door's knob. Later, you'll be able to switch doors if you want, but for now, consistency will help your dog learn faster.

C. Pick a cue for going outside. If you've already started using something like "wanna go outside?" you can continue. If not, pick something and make sure you and your family use it every time.

Now we're going to teach your dog to ring the bell to go outside. You'll notice these are the same steps we've already outlined for outdoor training. They're repeated here for your convenience—we're just adding a new cue!

Step 2:

A. Attach a leash to your dog. If you're not attached to your dog, you can't control the environment, so he could end up running all over your backyard!

B. Hide a couple of small treats in your hand. Make sure they're something he really likes.

Be careful what signal your dog uses to let you know that he has to eliminate—it may not translate well with other people or in other situations.

Step 3:

A. Approach the door. Gently take your dog's paw and gently ring the bell, saying your cue, "Wanna go outside?"

B. Immediately open the door and take your dog outside.

C. Watch your dog for signs he has to eliminate: sniffing the ground, assuming the position to go, etc. As soon as he starts, give him your cue to potty: "Go potty!" "Do your business!" Say whatever you want, just make sure you use the same cue every time.

D. When he's done, praise him! A simple "good dog" won't

Super Simple Tip

Puppies often have to eliminate twice in a row, so wait a few minutes before bringing your dog back inside.

cut it—make him know you're thrilled with his performance! Give him a cookie and tell him he's wonderful.

Helpful Hints:

- If you have a puppy, be advised that puppies often have to go twice. This means that Fido may pee or poop in one spot, then walk around a bit and pee and poop in another.
- Give your dog an allotted amount of time to find the right spot. If you want him to learn to do his business within five minutes, then only give him five minutes. Be consistent. Don't give him 30 minutes one Saturday, and then get frustrated when he takes 30 minutes Monday morning.

Some dogs may paw at the door when they want to go out.

Step 4:

A. If you want Fido to now play in his fenced yard, take off his leash and give him another cue, like "go play!" By making sure he potties first, he learns to get it out of the way before playtime. This comes in handy, especially when traveling or on bad weather days when he can't play outside! He'll learn to do his business quickly right off the bat.

B. If he does not go within your allotted time, bring him back inside and put him in his crate for 15 minutes. Then try again from Step 1. If he's confined, he will be less likely to have an accident in the house. If you're able to watch him very carefully, then you can do that, instead.

Step 5:

A. After a while, your dog will start ringing the bell on his own. You may find he doesn't use his paw but prefers to use his nose. This is fine! Once you teach

Some dogs are very clever and ring the bell so they can go out to play. Make sure that your pup knows that he's out there to eliminate, and reward him afterwards.

your dog the signal, it's important you respond to it. If he rings the bell and you're busy watching TV, he could have an accident inside if you don't let him out!

B. Another handy option when using a bell is that you can take it with you when you travel. If you bring your dog to a friend's house, you can put the bell on a door there. Your dog will be in a new place, but he'll have his old familiar signal! This means there will be less of a chance that he'll have accidents in your friend's place.

COMMON BELL TRAINING CHALLENGES

Here are some common challenges when training your dog to ring a bell to signal he needs to go out:

"My dog is afraid of the bell!"

Some dogs are sound sensitive and may be frightened by the bell sound. Some shy dogs may also be afraid of the bell just dangling from the door. If your dog is nervous about this in any way, then don't force him to ring the bell. You'll just make his fear worse!

A reward-based training class will help boost your dog's confidence, which may help him achieve housetraining success.

Instead, try leaving the bell on the door and just letting it ring when you open it. Your dog may get used to the sound. If this is even too much for your dog, you can try using a smaller bell or another, softer signal. Still too much? Then skip the bell idea, because you don't want him to be afraid to go outside! Consider taking your dog to a reward-based training class to boost his confidence.

"My dog learned to ring the bell all right; he rings it all the time! But when I take him outside, all he wants to do is play! Should I ignore him when he rings it and I know he doesn't have to potty?"

It's tempting, but no. If you do ignore him, then you may miss a real signal that he has to potty. It won't be fair to get angry with him if he told you he needed to go outside but you didn't respond. Instead, congratulate yourself on successfully teaching your dog that the bell is a signal to go outside! Your smart dog has figured out all he has to do is ring that bell and you jump to let him out. If it's any consolation, just about every dog reaches this conclusion sooner or later!

You can stay one step ahead of your dog. Remember how I told you to leash your dog when you take him outside? That's your ticket to less ringing in your ears. When Fido rings the bell, immediately put him on his leash and take him outside. If he doesn't potty but acts like he wants to play, then just bring him inside. After a couple of times, he'll realize it's no fun to ring the bell just to get a free pass to the outdoors.

"I like the idea, but I really don't want a bell hanging from my door. Is there another signal I can use?"

If you don't like the sharp ring of the bell, you could try the more soothing sounds of a small wind chime. If you don't like the looks of a bell hanging from the door, there are some products on the market that stay on the ground and simulate a doorbell. Some are even paw-shaped. You can train your dog to press on the object, and it rings a chime. Whatever signal you choose, just make sure it's not destructive and it's one you can live with for a long time.

Having a signal to go out will help your dog communicate with you more effectively.

Chapter 12

Advanced Training

As your training progresses, your dog can earn more and more freedom and privileges, because you'll be able to trust him in your home not to have accidents. But how do you know when to push forward?

It's tempting to rush ahead, because the early steps take some effort on your part. Sure, you'd rather open the door and let your dog run outside to potty on his own. And you really want to be able to leave him loose in your home when you run an errand. However, please make sure your dog is ready for these next steps before you try them. One of the biggest mistakes people make when housetraining their dogs is moving ahead too quickly, before their dogs are ready.

Until you feel he is ready, your dog should wear his collar and leash when brought outside to eliminate.

If you move forward too fast, you'll lose ground in training. Your dog will probably have accidents, which is just giving him a chance to practice eliminating in the house. You'll get frustrated because you thought you were making progress, and you and your dog will both be unhappy!

All training starts with baby steps, then moves on to more difficult steps as the subject gains knowledge. You didn't start learning advanced math in kindergarten—you had to learn what numbers were in the first place! You learned to recognize them, then to add and subtract them, then to multiply and divide them. Some of you may have even gone on to learn very complex mathematical formulas. But everyone starts with simple lessons and then builds on them. This is the best way to teach your dog, too. The training may seem to take longer, but it sticks better! Just think…start with a solid foundation and then build upon it, and you'll have a housetrained dog for a lifetime.

I'm now going to assume your dog is doing great so far, and you think he's ready to forge ahead. Here are some examples on how you can advance his training.

If you take your dog out on leash in his fenced yard and he promptly goes potty when you give him the cue…

Step 1:

A. Try taking him out on leash every other time for a couple of days. On the sessions with the leash, proceed as usual. On the tries without the leash, be sure to stay in the doorway and give him his cue to potty. Remember to always praise him when he goes!

B. If that's going well, then take your dog out on leash every third time for a couple of days. On the sessions with the leash, proceed as usual. On the tries without the leash, still stand in the doorway and give him his cue. Praise him when he goes!

C. If that's going well, then start taking him out on leash randomly. On the sessions with the leash, proceed as usual. On the tries without the leash, still stand in the doorway and give him his cue. Praise him when he goes!

Step 2:

This step will reduce your supervision when your dog is outside. Of course, if you prefer to stand there with your dog, by all means do so! But some folks would rather just let their dogs out and trust they're going to eliminate outside. This step is for them.

Gradually allow your dog access to more of your house by placing baby gates in doorways.

At this point, your dog should be going potty promptly each time, with and without the leash. If he sometimes wanders off leash all over the yard for 20 minutes before finding the perfect spot, you should back up your training and encourage him to succeed at Step 1 before moving forward.

A. Let your dog outside for a day or so while you stand in the doorway and give him his cue to potty. Praise him when he goes!

B. If this is going well, let your dog outside, stand in the doorway and give him his cue, and then go back inside. Peek through a window to make sure he eliminates. Go and get him, and then praise him. The next time,

If you are going to allow your dog to run off leash, make sure that he's in a fenced-in area.

stand in the doorway again. Randomly switch techniques.

C. If this is going well, you can let your dog outside and give him his cue. Congratulations! Your dog has learned to potty outside, quickly, without you having to watch him every second. Good job!

If he used to pee in his crate on his blanket so you took the blanket away, and he has not peed in his crate for two weeks straight…

Give him back his blanket, but only if he's not a destructive chewer and you know he'll be safe. If he continues to hold his urine with his blanket in the crate, great! If he pees on it again, take it away and wait a while longer before you try this again.

If your supervision and schedule are going wonderfully, and your dog has not had an accident in the house for two weeks straight…

This is great news. You deserve a pat on the back! If you want, you can start decreasing the amount of time you have to supervise your dog or confine him in his crate. There are a couple of things to watch, however. If you have a young puppy, then housetraining may not be the only reason you are crate training him. If he's destructive or likely to chew on things that may hurt him, then continue your crate training. Many puppies outgrow their destructive tendencies, although some adult dogs never do. If you have an adult dog that still loves to chew things up, then you may have to continue crating or confining him as well. It's important to keep your dog safe!

Super Simple Tip

For housetraining success, work in small steps to teach your dog what you want him to learn, and reward him for each achievement.

These steps assume your dog is not destructive or likely to hurt himself if left out of his crate for periods of time.

Step 1:

A. It's important you don't give your dog too much freedom all at once. Think about your daily routine and how you can work in a little less crate time. Let's say you always crate your dog when fixing dinner. One day, try leaving him outside the crate while you prepare the meal. Maybe you crate your dog while you get ready in the morning. You may try leaving him loose with you in the bedroom one morning instead. Pick a short time at first—it's not a good idea to leave him loose while you run to the store just yet!

B. Be sure to set your dog up for success! If the time period you choose is not near a typical potty break, give him an extra one right before you start your trial. That way, he'll have a chance to empty his bladder or bowels and be less likely to need to go during his new taste of increased freedom.

C. These steps still have you in the house with your dog. There's a big difference between leaving your dog loose while you're there and leaving him loose when you're out of the house! Some dogs do great when you're still there but break down when you pull out of the driveway. This is not unusual, so don't worry. You'll just have to keep your pace slow.

If this is going well, you can increase the time he spends outside the crate. If you find accidents, then you're just pushing your dog too fast. Go back a couple of steps and try again later.

Once your dog is housetrained, he can share your bedroom without making a mess.

Please don't be discouraged—this is normal!

Step 2:

This step is for folks who want to have their dogs loose in the bedroom with them at night. It's also for people who want their dogs to be loose in the house when they leave for errands or work.

    A. It's time to try leaving your dog out of his crate, unsupervised, for longer periods of time. This time you're going to leave the house. Keep times short at first, maybe 20 minutes. You can leave a peanut butter-stuffed chew toy with your dog as a treat to occupy him while you're gone.

    B. Don't give him the entire run of the house at first. If he's used to being in his crate, you can block off a room and leave his crate in there for him to get in if he wants. Limit his space and you'll have a greater chance of success!

Step 3:

A. If this is going well, you can continue to build up slowly. For example, if your dog does great for 20 minutes, see how he does for an hour or two. If that goes well, try a four-hour session. Still going well? You may want to try leaving your dog loose when you go to work all day, or if you want your dog to be loose in the bedroom, now's the time to try it.

B. If your dog is doing great confined in your kitchen with his crate, you can start giving him more room. Close off some doors or put up some baby gates to limit his space at first. You can decide how much room you want to give him as he continues to refrain from having accidents in your home.

C. If there are no accidents during this time, you're both doing great! If you find an accident, you'll have to back up your training and give your dog a chance to do well at the smaller steps before you tackle harder ones.

Celebrate each success—both you and your dog are making progess!

These are just a few examples of building on your housetraining efforts. You can build your own steps using these as a guideline. Think about your schedule and what you want your dog to accomplish. If it helps, write down your goals. Make sure they are realistic—can your dog really hold it as long as you want him to? Is your dog the right age to handle that much freedom? If so, then work gradually to reach your goals. Take small steps and make sure what you are teaching your dog is what he is learning. Celebrate each success, because both you and your dog are making progress! Understand there will be setbacks, and these are normal. But if you stick with the program and you're consistent and patient, you can successfully housetrain your dog. You can do it!

Chapter 13

Housetraining Problems

Throughout this book, I've highlighted common challenges you may encounter during each step of the housetraining process. However, there are other challenges that many dog owners come across during the overall process. Please don't feel bad if you're having trouble housetraining your dog. You're not alone! That's why I created this book, to help you through the process. You can do it!

Now, here's a troubleshooting section to help you with common housetraining problems.

<u>TOP 12 HOUSETRAINING PROBLEMS...AND HOW TO SOLVE THEM</u>

1. "I don't understand why my dog can hold it all night but can't go all day without peeing in the house. Is that normal?"

Yes. Think about your dog's activity at night—he's sleeping! The more active he is, the more his body processes nutrients, which means he has to eliminate. If your dog holds it all night but has accidents during the day, he's not being defiant or trying to make you angry. He can't help it physically. After all, we usually can hold it all night but take more potty breaks during the day, too!

Make sure you are confining your dog properly and holding realistic expectations on how long he can go without potty breaks. Remember, the more you let your dog have the chance to have accidents in the house, the more he's practicing that behavior. And practice makes perfect, so set your dog up for success! Supervise him closely, and when you can't, put him in his crate.

If your dog is having problems with housetraining, start at the beginning and try again.

2. "I let my dog outside for an hour, and the second he steps inside he pees on the floor! Is he being stubborn? Does he have an overactive bladder, or does he just not have a clue?"

He probably doesn't have a clue that you let him outside to potty. Instead, he thinks you let him outside to party! When you let a dog outside by himself, you're not giving him any direction. Even if you tell him, "Rover, go outside and potty!" he has no idea what these words mean. As a result, he's going to do doggie things, like chase butterflies, bark at the neighbors, smell the grass, and chase squirrels. There are a lot of interesting things to do outside, compared to inside your home. Then, when you finally bring him back inside, he suddenly realizes he has to pee! That's why you can let him out for an extended period of time, and he'll still pee on your rug soon after coming inside.

To fix this, follow my directions on how to housetrain your dog. This means you'll have to go outside with your dog, with your dog on-leash, until he gets used to the routine and no longer eliminates inside. I realize this can be a pain, especially in bad weather! But it's the easiest way for you to teach your dog what you want. Just think of all the carpet cleaning costs you'll save!

3. "My dog pees when I go to pet him. He pees when people come over or when he's greeting someone. I yell at him, but that just makes it worse. It's like he's overexcited...what can I do?"

This is actually not a housetraining problem. When a dog pees when you try to pet him or when you lean over him, it's called submissive urination. Don't let this go to your head, but your dog is actually trying to tell you that you are superior to him!

Dogs communicate very differently than humans. When a higher-ranking dog approaches a lower-ranking dog, the lower-ranking dog may pee to signal to the other dog that he respects him. He's acknowledging that he is lower down on the totem pole of leadership. The other dog recognizes this gesture as a sign of his upper status.

When you lean over your dog, you're actually making a dominant move. You're looming over your dog. In dog language, this is a very assertive position. If he pees at this time, he's trying to tell you that you outrank him. If you yell at him, he thinks you didn't get his message, so he'll pee more to try to get his message across.

Sometimes submissive urination is common in puppies, and they outgrow it. There are certain breeds that tend to have this problem more than others, such as Cocker Spaniels. You may find your dog only does it with certain people or certain types of people, like tall men or people with deep voices. Your dog is not being spiteful, nor is he stupid and unable to understand not to pee in the house. This is a completely different issue—it's one of communication.

Submissive urination is worse when you come home after being gone

Submissive urination can be common in puppies.

for a while. The next time you come home, then, completely ignore your dog. Don't talk to him, don't make eye contact with him, and don't pet him. Go about your business and settle in at home for about 15 minutes. Then, very casually, acknowledge your dog. Make it very matter-of-fact, because if you get excited, your dog will start peeing to greet you! Casually take your dog out to potty, giving him a chance to empty his bladder. Be sure to reward him when he goes outside. The calmer you are, the calmer he'll be. Then you can pet him and shower love on him. Do not loom over him to pet him. Instead, scrunch down and scratch him on the chest or under the chin, which is less threatening. Just don't crank up your enthusiasm, or your dog will feel a need to show you you're the boss again!

Teach your friends and family members the same routine. They should completely ignore your dog upon arrival until he calms down. Then they should scratch him under the chin or on his chest without looming over him.

With time, you'll notice your dog pees less and less when greeting people. He'll gain more confidence and control over his submissive bladder!

4. "My older dog was housetrained right from the minute I brought him home, but my new puppy is impossible! Why am I having so much trouble with this dog when my other dogs were so easy? Did I just end up with a dumb dog?"

Your dog is probably not dumb, he just learns things differently than your other dogs. Many people have fond memories of that perfect, once-in-a-lifetime gift of a dog: the dog that hardly ever did anything wrong, was absolutely brilliant and kind, and will always have a special place in our hearts. As dogs age and pass on, they can also take on the golden glow of selective memory…sometimes we forget that they did indeed have bad days in their youths, too!

Every dog is different and unique, with an individual personality. Even if you get littermates, a brother and sister can be as different as night and day! This is normal. Just as each dog is different, they learn differently, too. What comes easily to one dog may take another months to figure out. That doesn't mean one dog is dumber than another.

Your new dog will never be the old dog that you hold so dear. It's not fair to compare them, because the new guy will never match up to your memories. Besides, you can fix this! Just train your dog; then you can work on building special memories with him, too!

5. "I take my dog out on leash, but it takes him forever to find the perfect spot to go. Is there anything I can do to speed this process up? It's making me late for work!"

You have more control over this than you think. If you let your dog take 30 minutes to find the right spot, then you're teaching him to take 30 minutes to find the right spot. How much time do you want him to take? Only five or ten minutes? Then take him out on leash, give him the cue to potty, and give him your allotted amount of time. If he hasn't gone, bring him back inside and confine him in his crate for 15 minutes. Then try again. He'll soon learn he has a limited window to eliminate.

Sometimes this is only a problem in bad weather. Let's face it, we wouldn't want to do our business outside in the rain or snow, either! For this reason, please have some sympathy for your dog if he hesitates to go outside at these times. Just be kind but firm, and if he doesn't eliminate, then bring him back inside and confine him for 15 minutes, then try again. Give him an extra special treat when he does go outside in bad weather. It also wouldn't hurt to carry an umbrella!

6. "This is embarrassing, but my dog eats his stools. In fact, he eats my other dog's stools, too! Is there anything I can do to stop this disgusting habit?"

This is pretty gross, but it's also pretty common. Sometimes it's just a puppy thing, but it can be common in adult dogs, too. Some dogs just

Every dog is different and unique, with an individual personality.

love the taste of fresh poop. Awful, isn't it?

There are products you can purchase on the market that you add to your dog's food. They're supposed to make the stools taste bad, as if that makes any sense. Shouldn't they already taste horrible?! Some people rave about these products, but many folks don't have any luck with them.

Some also say that if you add pumpkin, pineapple, or some other food to your dog's dish, it'll produce the same effect. Again, there are mixed reviews about the success of this method.

There is a tried and true method that will stop your dog from eating poop. It's management. If you're outside with your dog on leash, he can't eat anything he's not supposed to because you can stop him. If you pick up your yard every day, then he also can't eat poop because there won't be any there to eat. Yes, this is a hassle, but it'll make your dog's kisses a lot sweeter, and it's much healthier for your dog.

Eating poop can make your dog very sick. If other animals get into your yard, like neighborhood cats, and your dog eats their poop, you have no idea what kind of nasties are getting into his system. Thus, if you have a dog that loves to dine on this disgusting dish, please pick up your yard every day. He can't possibly snack on poop if you effectively manage his environment so he never runs across any to eat.

7. "My dog only goes in the house when I'm not home. It's usually in my shoe, but he's even gone on my bed! Is he mad at me for leaving him at home?"

This can be a challenging concept for us, but dogs really aren't spiteful or stubborn creatures. They don't sit up all night, plotting ways to make your life miserable. Dogs live for the moment. If your dog gets into the trashcan and strews last night's dinner leftovers all over the kitchen, he didn't plan this out thoughtfully the week, the night, or even the minute before. He probably walked by the trashcan, smelled last night's pork chops, and went for them! If you yelled at him after he'd already done it, and he did it again the next day, he's not being spiteful or trying to show you he's boss. He's just remembering the sweet taste of those pork chops, and he thinks they may live in that trashcan!

When a dog pees on something personal, like your shoe or your bed, it could mean that he is upset about being left alone. He's not mad; he could be stressed. Some dogs get nervous when they're alone—dogs are pack animals, and many feel most comfortable when they're with their families. When we're stressed, we may reach for the ice cream or indulge in an alcoholic beverage. When dogs are stressed, some chew things to make themselves feel better, and some have accidents in the house. If they do miss you and are upset and stressed that you're gone, it makes sense to go to a place that smells the most like you. You wear your shoes all the time and you sleep in your bed, so those items hold a lot of your scent.

Super Simple Tip

Establishing a daily routine for your dog and sticking to it will help keep him from becoming stressed, which will lessen the chance of him having a housetraining accident.

This doesn't mean you should have your dog with you all the time. It would be great if life worked that way, but most people have to leave their dogs alone sometimes! Your dog must learn to be okay by himself.

If your dog is having accidents in the house, confine him when you're gone so he doesn't have a chance to practice this behavior. Make sure he has access to his favorite safe toys. Consider leaving the radio or television on as a comforting sound.

If your dog is showing signs of extreme stress, like chewing on your doorframe, leaving puddles of drool on the floor, or hurting himself in an attempt to get outside, then this could be a sign of true separation anxiety. If these symptoms sound familiar, please consult a professional dog trainer or applied animal behaviorist and your veterinarian.

8. "My dog sleeps with me, but he pees in the middle of the night when I'm sleeping. I'm always waking up to an accident on the floor. What can I do?"

Do you want your dog to sleep on the bed with you? As long as your dog has no aggression problems and is completely housetrained, then this is usually not a problem. But if your dog is peeing in the house, then he's not housetrained! If you're not confining him at night, you're setting him up to fail your housetraining program. Basically, you're giving him every chance to eliminate in the house. He'll never learn because you're teaching him it's okay to pee in the house. You can't correct him for eliminating in the house unless you catch him in the act—and you're fast asleep! And you can't get mad at him, because you're the one who's letting it happen! Oops!

The answer to your problem is good old-fashioned management. You need to confine him in his crate until he learns not to go in the house. When he's housetrained, then he can earn the privilege of sleeping in your bed. But the more mistakes you let him make, the longer it will take to fix the problem, because it's just too confusing for him. He thinks it's okay to pee in the house because no one is telling him immediately that it's wrong. He wakes up, gets on the floor, pees, hops back up on the bed, and snuggles in for the rest of the night.

Do both of you a favor. First, housetrain your dog. Then, if you want, you can let him sleep on your bed. Your dog will be better off because the rules will be clearer to him. You'll be better off, too, because you can once again walk around your bedroom barefoot!

9. "My dog has to hold the world record for speed peeing. I only turn my back for a second, and he hides behind the couch and pees! Is there a way to stop this?"

It's easy to say you need to watch your dog like a hawk, but it's a lot harder in practice, isn't it? Your dog doesn't understand he needs to go outside, but he has learned he needs to hide from you. Maybe someone in your home yelled at him or scared him when he was peeing in the house previously, so he learned to hide in an attempt to avoid punishment. Whatever the reason, you need to keep a better eye on Speedy so he no longer has a chance to practice this behavior.

First, make sure you're cleaning the spot with a proper cleanser. It should be an enzymatic cleanser or a special cleanser you can get through your veterinarian. It takes a pet-specific cleanser to completely clean the spot so your dog does not keep coming back to the spot again and again.

Next, if you have to fix dinner, do the dishes or go to the bathroom yourself, confine your dog. Put him in his crate until you can watch him again. If he's faster than that, put him on leash, then tie the leash to your waist—you can pull it through your belt loop and secure it. You may feel a bit silly at first, being attached to your dog! But what a great way to really supervise him! You'll learn his body signals for when he has to eliminate. And you'll be able to catch him having an accident right when it starts, because he won't be able to dart behind the couch.

You won't have to stay attached to your dog forever. The more you learn to read your dog so you can rush him outside and reward him when he goes there, the more that will become a habit for him. He'll learn you want him to eliminate outside, instead of behind the couch, because you'll be on top of the situation every time—literally!

10. "My dog goes potty in the crate. Is the crate too big?"

Maybe. But there are a couple of factors that could cause your puppy to eliminate in his crate.

Are you sure you're not leaving your dog in the crate too long? In general, puppies four months and younger can only go a few hours without needing a potty break. Puppies six months can hold it about six or seven hours. Adult dogs can usually go eight to nine hours without a potty break. First, make sure you have realistic expectations about how long your puppy can stay in his crate without needing to relieve himself. If you're not waiting too long to let your puppy out, then the crate may be too big. If your puppy can potty in his crate and still remain high and dry, then the crate is too large to effectively teach him housetraining. Dogs should just be able to stand up, stretch out and turn around in their crates when you are housetraining them.

If your dog is having accidents in the house, confine him when you're gone so that he doesn't have a chance to practice this behavior.

So you may need a smaller crate, or a divider to make the crate smaller. With growing puppies, always pay attention to their crates to make sure they are not too small. What's perfect one month for housetraining may be way too small the next month!

Are you leaving a blanket or bedding in the crate? Some dogs will pee on the blanket, ball it up in the corner and keep dry. If this is your problem, then simply remove the blanket. Once your dog is housetrained, then you can add the blanket back. Removing bedding is also a good idea if you have a puppy that loves to chew on everything! Some puppies, or even older dogs that are big chewers, can shred a blanket to ribbons. Some will even eat the pieces, which can cause a serious medical emergency. If you've tried all these things and you continually come home to a puppy that has peed and/or pooped all over his crate, then take your puppy to your veterinarian to rule out a medical problem. Your puppy may have something wrong where he cannot hold his bladder or bowels for a reasonable amount of time.

Another thing to consider is your puppy's early training. Was he raised in a cage? Or maybe outdoors only, in a small pen or kennel? If your puppy was restricted during his early weeks so he could not move away from his "den" to eliminate, then he may have learned it's okay to be around his waste. This is not his fault! His breeder gave him this problem, and now you have to undo the damage. Review our chapter on Housetraining—it covers tips on how to deal with this special challenge.

11. "My dogs were fine in the old house, but we recently moved. Now I'm finding accidents on the carpet. What could be the problem?"

Moving into a new home can be stressful for the entire family. That includes your dogs! It's a new environment, a new routine…when dogs are stressed, one of the ways they sometimes show it is by having accidents in the house. You may notice other odd behavioral issues, too. Some dogs that always got along start to scrap with each other. Some dogs that never chewed up a thing at the old house suddenly turn into sharks and tear things up at the new house. These can all be signs of stress.

Dogs also don't generalize very well. Information they learn in one location doesn't always transfer right away to a new location.

The good news is you can solve this problem. Just start your housetraining from scratch. Review your training with your dogs so they get into a routine again. This will remind them what your expectations are, so you can all enjoy your new home together.

12. "My dog used to be house-trained, but suddenly he's been peeing inside again. Is he mad at me? He used to be so reliable!"

Any time you have a sudden change in behavior, it's a good idea to consult your veterinarian to make sure there isn't a physical problem that's causing it. If your dog has been perfectly housetrained for some time, then suddenly starts peeing in the house again, he may have a urinary tract infection or another physical problem.

If your veterinarian says your dog is healthy, then take a look at your environment. Is there anything unusual going on? Any visitors staying with you for a while? Has a beloved child taken off for college? Any new additions to the family? How about any fighting going on?

Your dog is very in tune to your family, and he's also a creature of routine. Dogs love routines! When things are out of whack at home, it can be very stressful for your dog. One way a dog shows stress is by having accidents in the house.

Let's say you and your spouse are under stress and have been arguing about money. The next day, you find pee in the dining room. Maybe you brought a new kitten into your home…and you then find dog poop in your bedroom. These could be signs that your dog is picking up tensions in your house or is stressed about what's going on. If you think this might be the case, try and keep your dog to his routine as much as possible. Take him for extra walks and fun, reward-based training sessions. He's part of your family, and when your family's upset or running mad like a three-ring circus, he is, too!

If your dog is having accidents in the house, clean the spot with an enzymatic or special cleanser.

Conclusion

Once you realize that you can set goals for your dog and reach them, your relationship will improve dramatically! You won't have to come home all upset and angry because you've found an accident on the floor. You won't be embarrassed when your friends come over because your carpet smells like urine. And the simplest concept of all is that you hold the power to change your dog's behavior. You can make it worse or you can make it better—and I've given you the information you need to make it much, much better!

By setting realistic expectations, using consistent rules, being patient, and using reward-based methods, you'll achieve housetraining success! Once you realize how to effectively train your dog, maybe you won't stop there. Just think of the possibilities!

Dogs compete in a variety of fun sports; they track and find people, and they give comfort to folks in nursing homes, children's' hospitals, and other healthcare facilities. Whether you want to pursue any of these activities with your dog or just keep him all to yourself as your best buddy, this is an important step in your relationship. By taking the time and effort to housetrain your dog, you're helping him be a better family companion…for life.

ASSOCIATIONS AND ORGANIZATIONS

Breed Clubs

American Kennel Club (AKC)
5580 Centerview Drive
Raleigh, NC 27606
Telephone: (919) 233-9767
Fax: (919) 233-3627
E-mail: info@akc.org
www.akc.org

Canadian Kennel Club (CKC)
89 Skyway Avenue, Suite 100
Etobicoke, Ontario M9W 6R4
Telephone: (416) 675-5511
Fax: (416) 675-6506
E-mail: information@ckc.ca
www.ckc.ca

Federation Cynologique Internationale (FCI)
Secretariat General de la FCI
Place Albert 1er, 13
B – 6530 Thuin
Belqique
www.fci.be

The Kennel Club
1 Clarges Street
London
W1J 8AB
Telephone: 0870 606 6750
Fax: 0207 518 1058
www.the-kennel-club.org.uk

United Kennel Club (UKC)
100 E. Kilgore Road
Kalamazoo, MI 49002-5584
Telephone: (269) 343-9020
Fax: (269) 343-7037
E-mail: pbickell@ukcdogs.com
www.ukcdogs.com

Rescue Organizations and Animal Welfare Groups

American Humane Association (AHA)
63 Inverness Drive East
Englewood, CO 80112
Telephone: (303) 792-9900
Fax: 792-5333
www.americanhumane.org

American Society for the Prevention of Cruelty to Animals (ASPCA)
424 E. 92nd Street
New York, NY 10128-6804
Telephone: (212) 876-7700
www.aspca.org

Royal Society for the Prevention of Cruelty to Animals (RSPCA)
Telephone: 0870 3335 999
Fax: 0870 7530 284
www.rspca.org.uk

The Humane Society of the United States (HSUS)
2100 L Street, NW
Washington DC 20037
Telephone: (202) 452-1100
www.hsus.org

Therapy

Delta Society
875 124th Ave NE, Suite 101
Bellevue, WA 98005
Telephone: (425) 226-7357
Fax: (425) 235-1076
E-mail: info@deltasociety.org
www.deltasociety.org

Therapy Dogs Incorporated
PO Box 5868
Cheyenne, WY 82003
Telephone: (877) 843-7364
E-mail: therdog@sisna.com
www.therapydogs.com

Therapy Dogs International (TDI)
88 Bartley Road
Flanders, NJ 07836
Telephone: (973) 252-9800
Fax: (973) 252-7171
E-mail: tdi@gti.net
www.tdi-dog.org

Training

Association of Pet Dog Trainers (APDT)
150 Executive Center Drive Box 35
Greenville, SC 29615
Telephone: (800) PET-DOGS
Fax: (864) 331-0767
E-mail: information@apdt.com
www.apdt.com

National Association of Dog Obedience Instructors (NADOI)
PMB 369
729 Grapevine Hwy.
Hurst, TX 76054-2085
www.nadoi.org

Veterinary and Health Resources

American Animal Hospital Association (AAHA)
P.O. Box 150899
Denver, CO 80215-0899
Telephone: (303) 986-2800
Fax: (303) 986-1700
E-mail: info@aahanet.org
www.aahanet.org/index.cfm

American College of Veterinary Internal Medicine (ACVIM)
1997 Wadsworth Blvd., Suite A
Lakewood, CO 80214-5293
Telephone: (800) 245-9081
Fax: (303) 231-0880
Email: ACVIM@ACVIM.org
www.acvim.org

American College of Veterinary Ophthalmologists (ACVO)
P.O. Box 1311
Meridian, Idaho 83860
Telephone: (208) 466-7624
Fax: (208) 466-7693
E-mail: office@acvo.com
www.acvo.com

American Holistic Veterinary Medical Association (AHVMA)
2218 Old Emmorton Road
Bel Air, MD 21015
Telephone: (410) 569-0795
Fax: (410) 569-2346
E-mail: office@ahvma.org
www.ahvma.org

American Veterinary Medical Association (AVMA)
1931 North Meacham Road – Suite 100
Schaumburg, IL 60173
Telephone: (847) 925-8070
Fax: (847) 925-1329
E-mail: avmainfo@avma.org
www.avma.org

ASPCA Animal Poison Control Center
1717 South Philo Road, Suite 36
Urbana, IL 61802
Telephone: (888) 426-4435
www.aspca.org

British Veterinary Association (BVA)
7 Mansfield Street
London
W1G 9NQ
Telephone: 020 7636 6541
Fax: 020 7436 2970
E-mail: bvahq@bva.co.uk
www.bva.co.uk

Canine Eye Registration Foundation (CERF)
VMDB/CERF
1248 Lynn Hall
625 Harrison St.
Purdue University
West Lafayette, IN 47907-2026
Telephone: (765) 494-8179
E-mail: CERF@vmbd.org
www.vmdb.org

Orthopedic Foundation for Animals (OFA)
2300 NE Nifong Blvd
Columbus, Missouri 65201-3856
Telephone: (573) 442-0418
Fax: (573) 875-5073
Email: ofa@offa.org
www.offa.org

PUBLICATIONS

Books

Anderson, Teoti. Terra-Nova *Puppy Care & Training*. Neptune City: T.F.H. Publications, 2007.

Morgan, Diane. *Good Dogkeeping*. Neptune City: TFH Publications, 2005.

WEBSITES

www.nylabone.com
www.tfh.com

Photo Credits

Nylabone® Cares.

Millions of dogs of all ages, breeds, and sizes have enjoyed our world-famous chew bones—but we're not just bones! Nylabone®, the leader in responsible animal care for over 50 years, devotes the same care and attention to our many other award-winning, high-quality, innovative products. Your dog will love them — and so will you!

Toys   Treats   Chews   Crates   Grooming